Reconciled by the Light

BOOK II

SPIRIT MESSAGES FROM A TEEN SUICIDE

ADVENTURES OF A PSYCHIC MEDIUM

i

Reconciled by the Light

Book II

Spirit Messages from a Teen Suicide

Adventures of a Psychic Medium

Ron Pappalardo

*Dedicated to the One
who has always
been there for me*

Acknowledgements

If I said thank you to all the people I am grateful to for playing a part in bringing this book to fruition, the list might be longer than the book itself. I do want to mention a few names, and if I've inadvertently left someone out, I implore your forgiveness.

The Rev. David and Takeko Hose provided the foundation for much of my spiritual growth, by having the courage to speak truth as they saw it, and graciously sharing it with anyone who wanted to receive it.

Philip Burley, a gifted medium with over twenty years of practice, instilled in me the confidence to move forward.

The Rev. Connie Graddy taught me the fundamentals of mediumship and opened my eyes to the broader world of Spiritualism.

Dale Graff made me aware of my psychic abilities and showed me how they work.

Patricia Titus made it possible for me to graduate from the Morris Pratt Institute's Course on Modern Spiritualism.

Nadia Pappalardo and Alice Osborn edited the manuscript and provided invaluable guidance and advice.

Mike and Irene McGarvie helped me navigate the waters of the publishing world.

The core members of my Spirit Circle – Greg Blakeney, Dr.Denise Heflin, Prof. Toni Brown, Alma Palmer, and several others, who have always loved and encouraged me.

Last but not least, Connie, my wife and partner of thirty plus years, with whom I continue to share the journey.

TABLE OF CONTENTS

INTRODUCTION

It seems that everyone's life is full of challenges. The biggest challenge of my life presented itself when I lost my first-born son, Joshua, to suicide when he was seventeen. That event catapulted me onto an emotional roller coaster-like journey that has been going on for several years now. It continues to this day, but the peaks and valleys of the roller coaster have slowly diminished. The ride is now a peaceful one. It feels more like a cruise ship sailing through the Inside Passage of Alaska than a roller coaster. The water is very placid there and each succeeding view—whether of a whale, a mountain, or a glacier—is more breathtaking than the previous one.

Unlike sailing on a cruise ship, my journey involves encounters in the world of spirit, a vast dimension beyond the boundaries of the five physical senses. After my son took his life, I was determined to find him on "the other side." I was determined to provide him with any assistance that I possibly could from the land of the living. In a matter of a few days, I was able to make contact with him with the help of some very gifted psychics and mediums. Over the next few years, I received extraordinary "letters" from him in which he described what happened to him when he entered the spirit world, who he met, and what his life is like there. Later, I began to experience the spirit world directly, as I received training and developed my own psychic abilities. So, a journey that began with heart-wrenching agony has now become one of awe-inspiring discovery. You can read the "letters" from Joshua, and the account of how I found him, in my first book, *Reconciled by the Light: the After-Death Letters from a Teen Suicide.*

I think everyone has had encounters of a psychic nature. Perhaps you have had the experience of having a person pop into your mind. Then your phone rings, and the person you were just thinking about is on the other end of the call. You might have had the experience of sensing the presence of a departed loved one. Many people have reported seeing a family member at the foot of their bed in a visitation only to find out the next day that their loved one has recently died. Maybe you've had a very vivid dream that you knew somehow was more than just a dream.

Then there are the phenomena of Near Death Experiences (NDEs). Countless people have been clinically dead—heart stopped, no brain activity—only to revive again with stories of how they went through a tunnel, entered a world of brilliant white light and all-encompassing love, and visited with deceased family members, religious figures, and even God.

All of these experiences, and innumerable others, point to the existence of a spirit world, life after death, or what psychic researchers refer to as "survivability."

This book recounts the journey I traveled after my son died that led me to discover the vast network of individuals and groups that engage in spirit communication. With their guidance and inspiration, I went through a long process of developing my own psychic abilities. After years of study and practice, I have now joined the ranks of the psychic mediums. I have had the honor and privilege of being an instrument to help people communicate with loved ones on the other side. In this book, we will explore these intriguing phenomena, not in the style of a textbook, but in an easy to read format based on personal experiences—most of them being my own.

In my view, the most important goal of studying spiritual phenomena should be the personal growth and development of the person doing the studying. We are not meant to just be entertained by the wonders of the spirit world; we are meant to use our understanding and experiences to improve ourselves and the world around us. Sadly, even practicing Spiritualists sometimes lose sight of this goal. It is easy to get caught up in the fascinating spiritual phenomena themselves and get distracted from our ultimate destination: reconciliation and union with our Divine Source.

Although I will reveal many spiritual experiences that in themselves are incredibly intriguing, fascinating, and astounding, the purpose of this book is to offer the reader encouragement and a pathway to develop your own psychic abilities. The ultimate goal of this development is having your own personal, direct encounter with Divine Spirit, God, the Creative Intelligence, or whatever name you want to give to the Source from which we all derive our life, love, and meaning.

The beauty and power of having a personal mystical experience with the Divine lies in the fact that it takes you from the state of belief or faith to the state of *knowing*. It reminds me of what the famous psychiatrist Carl Jung once said when a BBC interviewer asked him if he believed in God. He responded, "I don't need to believe; I know." When you have this experience, no one can take it away from you—it is yours forever. It is my sincerest hope that this book will help countless people find this experience.

PART I ADVENTURES IN PSYCHIC DEVELOPMENT

1 BACK TO AMERICA

As the British Airways jet that Connie and I were on took off from Heathrow Airport, the feelings within me were mixed; leaving England was a bittersweet experience. On one hand, I had a renewed sense of urgency to return home to the United States and quickly finish my first book, *Reconciled by the Light: the After-Death Letters from a Teen Suicide*. On the other hand, I was saddened to leave such a magical land.

For me, the British Isles have long been a "mother lode" of spiritual treasures. From the Celtic mysticism of pre-history to the extraordinary phenomena surrounding the appearance of Modern Spiritualism in the nineteenth century, Britain occupies a special place in my mind and heart.

As the airplane ascended above the English countryside, I looked out my window and was visually reminded how old this land is. Unlike the farmlands of the American plains states, with their checkerboard pattern of precisely one-mile-square layouts and their perfect north-south, east-west axes, the fields below me spread out like a giant amoeba. Stone walls, hedges, and narrow lanes meandered haphazardly through the countryside, their curving signatures following ancient paths that were set down in a time when most travel was done on foot.

As beautiful and intriguing as England is, with its rolling green fields, its Gothic churches, and its Roman ruins, the thing that attracts me the most is its spiritual heritage. Great Britain has blessed the world by producing many individuals with exceptional gifts and insights. Three of my favorites are Charles Dickens, Sir Arthur Conan Doyle, and Daniel Dunglas Home.

As a writer, Charles Dickens had an uncanny ability to demonstrate how inspiring human beings can be when they follow the "better angels" of their nature. The story of Ebenezer Scrooge illustrates how the inherent goodness that lies within every human being is unleashed when the heart is awakened through spiritual

4

realization. In perhaps his most beloved book, *A Christmas Carol,* the story revolves around spiritual communication between Scrooge and the ghosts of his deceased partners, the Marley brothers. Scrooge experiences a rebirth in his soul through encounters with the Ghosts of Christmas Past, Present, and Future and is transformed from a self-centered miser to a caring benefactor of his employees and neighbors.

Sir Arthur Conan Doyle is well-known as the author of the *Sherlock Holmes* mysteries, but few people know that he is considered the "St. Paul of Modern Spiritualism." A less publicized passion of his was teaching people about the spirit world. Conan Doyle has made an immeasurable contribution to our understanding of the phenomena of spirit communication. Among his other books on the subject, he is the author of a two-volume work, *The History of Spiritualism,* which provides a comprehensive account of the Spiritualist movement beginning with its birth in 1848 and bringing the reader up to the time of its publishing in 1926.

Daniel Dunglas Home was a Scottish medium known for his ability to levitate. Conan Doyle noted the unusual fact that Home could perform four separate types of mediumship: direct voice, trance speech, clairvoyance, and physical mediumship. Regarding Home's gifts as a physical medium, which included the movement of objects without touching them and levitating in and out of windows, Conan Doyle said Home had no equal. Home's abilities convinced countless members of the nineteenth century elite that there is far more to life than the struggles surrounding the material aspect of our existence. He performed séances for many of the crown heads of Europe, including Napoleon III, Queen Sophia of the Netherlands, and Tsar Nicholas II. The eminent British scientist Sir William Crookes, who confirmed Home's gifts while finding no evidence of fraud, made an exhaustive investigation of Home's abilities.

Dickens, Doyle, and Home appeared on the scene like modern-day prophets. They remind me that at its most essential core, life is a spiritual endeavor; they inspire me by demonstrating that a single individual can be a powerful force for goodness in society if he stays true to his convictions.

The plane leveled off at a very high altitude, and my wife Connie and I relaxed into the seats, lost in our own thoughts. Our trip to England had been a celebration of our 25th wedding anniversary. We had spent a wonderful few days wandering the streets of London together and visiting with friends, but for me the most intriguing experience was my visit to the Wimbledon Spiritualist Church.

"What a shame." I thought. "I wish I could find a Spiritualist community in North Carolina!"

2 EUREKA! I'VE FOUND IT!

"What in the world is that?" I asked out loud. Alone in my car, no one could hear me.

I was driving out from Durham, North Carolina on US Highway 15/501, about 10 miles north of the city in the Piedmont countryside near the tiny rural community of Bahama when I saw the unusual sign on the right side of the road. If you thought Bahama was named after some island in the Caribbean, you would be wrong. First of all, the town is pronounced Buh-HAY-muh; it got its name long ago by combining the first two letters in the names of three prominent families: the Balls, the Harrises, and the Mangums. The area is a bastion of Methodists and Southern Baptists, which made the sign seem all the more unusual.

"First United Metaphysical Chapel? I wonder what kind of church *that* is." The building was painted completely white. A large graceful statue of a beautiful angel stood out front. I speculated that it might be one of the New Thought denominations that sprang up in the late nineteenth century. I am always interested in investigating new religious movements, but while I was curious, I didn't plan to visit this one anytime soon. Little did I know that this was the type of group I had been trying to find for decades.

When a friend later informed me that this church conducted services that included mediumship, like the one I had experienced in England, I hastened to visit there the very next Sunday. It was August of 2008; about five months had passed since my return from London and my visit to the Wimbledon Spiritualist Church on Easter Sunday. Just as my friend said, the service was similar to the British one and did indeed include messages from those in the spirit world.[i]

There were a few differences, though; I encountered the first one immediately as I walked through the front door. A woman greeted me and handed me a small piece of paper that she called a "billet." It was about the size of a small napkin and had three numbers typed on it.

"On these three lines, write down the names of people in spirit that you would like to get a message from," she said. "Down here," she said, pointing to the area underneath the three lines, "you can write a question you'd like to get an answer to. Then, fold it over so no one can see what you've written inside, and write your initials and birthday on the outside. Later in the service, an usher will come by and collect all the billets."

I went into the sanctuary, which was a barrage of white—white walls, white furniture, white chairs—even the carpet was white. Two islands of color were the tall arrangements of roses that stood at the front on either side of the podium. Out of the corner of my eye, I caught sight of a large framed portrait hanging on the left front wall. It was a print of an old painting of Jesus, perhaps a hundred years old. His benevolent face was surrounded by a glowing aura of light, and I found the presence of this portrait comforting.

"If they've got a picture of Jesus here, they can't be *that* crazy," I thought.

The congregation was very small, no more than a couple of dozen people. The service began with something I'd never seen before. They called it the "Healing Service." A few chairs had been placed on either side of the front of the sanctuary. The main Healing Minister, an elderly woman with elegantly-styled white hair, conducted this part of the ministration. At an appointed time she announced, "Anyone who would like to receive a healing may come forward now. The healers are ready."

Healing ministers were now standing behind each of the chairs, and one by one, a few people got up from the congregation and took a seat in one of them. I was fascinated as I turned my attention to one of the healers—we'll call her Clara—as she held her hands just above the head of a middle-aged man sitting in her chair, wearing a focused but reverential look on her face. After a minute or so, she shifted the position of her hands. She held one in front of his heart, while she laid the other hand on his right shoulder. When she seemed to sense that one particular spot might require more healing energy than another, she shifted the position of her hands accordingly. She spent about five minutes with each congregant and then whispered, "God Bless you," to them, which was a signal that the healing was complete and that the recipient should leave the chair for the next person to come up.

I've had many opportunities to experience these healing chairs, both as a receiver and giver of healing. You can feel heat coming from the healers' hands. Sometimes it can be so hot you're convinced there must be some electrical apparatus involved. The

8

feeling is so soothing that you don't want the experience to end, and it's with reluctance that you leave the chair when it's over.

The rest of the service was not unlike a Sunday Service you might experience at a typical Protestant church, the singing of hymns, prayers, and a sermon, but it's what happened after the sermon that amazed me the most.

3 "SEEING" THE DEAD

"It's time for the Message Service," announced an African-American gentleman standing at the podium in an exquisitely tailored suit. He in turn introduced a middle-aged woman – we'll call her Joanie – who stood up and performed a demonstration of *clairvoyance*. The word *clairvoyance* literally means "seeing clearly" in French.

The most impressive thing about her messages was that she would often receive specific names or other verifiable information. In a typical exchange she would say something like this:

"I'm getting the name 'James.' Can anyone take the name 'James?'"

Someone in the audience would raise their hand; then she'd speak specifically to that person. What blew my mind even further is what would happen when two or more people raised their hand in response to the same name. Then she would say:

"Let me see if I can get a second name to go with 'James'… Okay, give me a moment … Can anybody take 'Martha' to go with 'James?'"

Then all of the people who had raised their hand for 'James' would lower them except for one. Joanie would then know that the message was meant for the one remaining person whose hand was still raised.

Later, if I spoke to the person who received the message I would be even more astounded.

"Excuse me, can you tell me who this person 'James' was?"

"Oh yes," they'd reply. "That was my great-uncle."

"And what about Martha, do you know who 'Martha' was?"

"Of course! That was my great-aunt, James' wife."

It's one thing for a medium to state that they are receiving a message from someone named James; it's quite another to receive a James and a Martha together and have the recipient confirm that they were a married couple related to them.

This very specific type of information received during a reading or message from spirit is what is called *evidentiary* material. I will talk more about evidentiary information in a later chapter. Suffice it to say that I take any spirit message with a huge "grain of salt" unless it includes evidentiary material, and I recommend others to do so as well.

* * *

When I was studying to expand my own mediumship abilities, I had a fascinating experience surrounding this whole issue of receiving names. I had begun attending something called a "Development Circle," which was usually led by the pastor. As the name implies, it's a meeting for people who are interested in developing their own psychic powers. During one of these sessions early on in my development, I was practicing giving messages to the other participants in the circle. As I stood up to begin, I received an unusual name. I could see the letters clearly spelled out in my mind's eye: K-e-l-v-i-n. Now Kelvin is not a common name, so I thought I wasn't "seeing" the letters properly; I thought spirit[ii] must have been trying to give me the name "Kevin." So I said:

"Can anyone take the name 'Kevin?'"

Nobody raised his or her hand.

I closed my eyes and again I saw the name Kelvin again, but this time the "L" was bigger than the other letters, kind of like this— K-e-**L**-v-i-n.

Now I knew that one of the ladies present had a husband named Kelvin, but I also knew he was still *alive,* so I thought, "I can't be getting a message from *that* Kelvin, can I?" Confused, I said:

"Can anyone take the name 'Kelvin?'"

Sure enough, Kelvin's wife raised her hand. Immediately, in my mind's eye I saw a large man wearing bib overalls.

"Does he ever wear bib overalls?" I asked.

"That's about all he ever wears!" she said.

As it turned out, Kelvin was a very large man who did landscaping for a living; one could usually find him riding around on a lawn mower wearing bib overalls.

Still sensing his presence, I somehow knew that Kelvin wanted me to pass on a simple message. "He just wants me to tell you that he loves you," I said.

Then I turned to the pastor and asked her what was going on? How could I receive a spirit message from someone who was still *alive*?

The pastor asked Kelvin's wife, "Where's Kelvin right now?"

"He's at home, sleeping," she replied.

"Well, that makes sense. Sometimes when people are sleeping, their spirit leaves their body and they can travel around and visit people. I guess Kelvin was just thinking about you and wanted to drop in and let you know he loves you," she said laughing.

4 "FEELING" THE DEAD

After Joanie finished with her demonstration of clairvoyance, it was time for the billet reading. The usher had collected all the little slips of paper into a straw offering basket and brought them up to the podium. Then Joanie picked up one of the billets and read the initials and birth date on the outside. That person raised their hand to let Joanie know that it was their billet. Then Joanie held the billet between the palms of her hands, closed her eyes, and concentrated.

The clairvoyance part of the message service had been conducted without the use of anything other than the medium's mind. There were no cards, crystal balls, or any other tools to assist her. Billet reading is a form of mediumship that comes under the classification of spiritual phenomena called *psychometry*. In *psychometry*, the medium does use a tool to assist the communication with spirit. The medium touches something, usually a physical object like a piece of clothing, a photograph, or jewelry belonging to the deceased person. Through that touch, the medium connects to the energy vibration of that person.

A good example is the experience Connie and I had with the medium Ann Poole at the Rhine Research Center. That experience is recounted in *Reconciled by the Light: the After-Death Letters from a Teen Suicide*. [iii] In that instance, Ann used a photograph of our son Joshua to pick up his vibration through *psychometry*; I handed her the photo, and before I had even returned to my seat she had already discerned that he had died through suicide, just by holding the picture in her hands.

Oftentimes during billet reading, the medium will perform a physical movement, rubbing the billet paper back and forth between the palms of the hands. When I began doing billet readings myself, I noticed that I often have a different experience than when I'm practicing straight clairvoyance. In *clairvoyance*, I "see" spiritually. Images will pop into my mind that convey information. These images might be of an actual object that has particular significance to the deceased person. Or they might be images that have *symbolic* meaning. For example, I once saw a conductor waving his baton in front of an orchestra. At first, I thought I was seeing an actual spirit and attempted to identify it. As the vision in my mind unfolded, however, I began to realize that the conductor was a symbol of my client. It represented his ability to harmonize the various people and other factors affecting his job performance. At other times I will see letters spelling out someone's name or a particular word.

However, in billet reading, I often "feel" the information rather than "see" it. Oftentimes the billet will feel warm, sometimes very warm. Then I might start to choke up if I perceive that the spirit trying to communicate felt a lot of love or deep connection to the person I'm giving the message to. So for me, billet reading can often be more of an emotional experience than clairvoyance.

The experience of picking up feelings or emotions comes under the umbrella of something called *clairsentience*. *Clairsentience* means "feeling clearly" in French. So for me, billet reading is a type of psychic reading that is often mostly *clairsentient*.

One of the most astounding experiences I've had receiving a billet reading was during a Mother's Day message service at the Metaphysical Chapel. I had decided to go sit in a healing chair during the beginning part of the service. From the chair I was sitting in, I was looking right at the big bouquets of roses that were arranged around the podium. My mother's name happens to be Rose. While I was sitting there, it dawned on me that even though it was Mother's Day, I hadn't even thought about my own mother even once that day. So, as I relaxed into the warmth of the healing hands, I started talking to my mom in my mind:

"Mom, it's Mother's Day, and I'm sorry I haven't even wished you a 'Happy Mother's Day' yet. I want you to know that I think you were a great mom; I always felt loved by you and you were such a bright spot in my childhood. Thank you for your great love. I wish I could give you all of these beautiful roses here in the church!"

The healer behind my healing chair finished and whispered "God Bless You," so I got up and returned to my pew. Later in the service, the Pastor was doing the billet readings. She picked up my billet and said:

"The first thing I get is 'Rose,'" she said. "This is your mom."

Then she said something that made my jaw drop.

"Did you send her flowers?"

14

"Yes," I said.

"Well, she wants you to know that she received all the flowers, and she's wearing one of them right now pinned to her breast," she said.

This experience impressed upon me the powerful effect sending thoughts and feelings towards deceased relatives and others in the spirit world can have. Our loved ones can sense these intentions; they can experience great joy and comfort when we send positive, loving thoughts and prayers their way.

5 "Painting" the Dead

After the service, Joanie stood in the lobby to greet each congregant as they departed the sanctuary. She told me that she was filling in for the pastor who was traveling and told me that the pastor is a far more impressive medium than Joanie is. She encouraged me to come again, and I promised I would. She also told me about the development classes that the church conducted every Wednesday night that gave people an opportunity to practice mediumship themselves. I got very excited about that and told her I'd be interested in checking that out.

I told her I had been searching for a group like this for many years and was so happy to have discovered one in the area. I went home inspired and full of wonder and anticipation.

One of the things I wondered about was how in the world a spiritualist church got established in the heart of the Bible Belt. I discovered later that The First United Metaphysical Chapel in Bahama had been founded just a few years earlier by a handful of elderly women from Indiana; some of them had moved to the South to be closer to children and grandchildren. Homesick for their church, and not being able to find one like it in North Carolina, they decided to go ahead and start one themselves. Indiana is a state that has a long tradition of being a leading center of Spiritualism. Spiritualists formed an Association there in 1886 and still operate a large center for the practice of mediumship near Indianapolis called Camp Chesterfield.

When I returned the following Sunday, the pastor gave the billet readings and just as Joanie had said she would, gave some very impressive messages. After the service, the pastor showed me an astounding "painting" hanging on the wall of the church library that she had brought with her when she moved from Indiana. It was a portrait of a beautiful young woman dressed in early twentieth century clothing. She looked beatific and had a peaceful, serene expression on her face. Although the pastor called it a painting, there were no brush strokes to be found anywhere on the original work. I could see some brush strokes on the woman's dress near the bottom of the painting, but the pastor explained that someone had added these later to touch up small areas where the original "paint" had flaked off. The young woman had died years before the painting was created, and the painting itself had been produced by the spirit world.

"This was received by the Bangs sisters," she explained.

"What kind of paint is that?" I asked.

"Nobody knows exactly what it is," she replied. "Painting experts have tried to figure it out, but all they can tell us is it's similar to the powder found on butterflies' wings."

The Bangs sisters were Mary and Elizabeth Bangs, two famous mediums of the late nineteenth and early twentieth centuries. Beginning in 1894 and continuing for more than 20 years, the Bangs sisters produced "precipitated" spirit paintings. They would sit on either side of a blank canvas without touching it. A painting of someone from the spirit world would then slowly appear—someone unknown to the Bangs sisters but recognizable to the client requesting the painting. Many of these paintings reside in a museum at Camp Chesterfield.[iv]

I had no intention of joining The First United Metaphysical Chapel, or any church for that matter, but I unexpectedly found myself doing so, following what I believed to be guidance coming from above. I also joined the Wednesday night Development Circle, and it was there that my spiritual senses began to really open up.

6 Developing my Spiritual Senses

"Just stand up, and see if you get anything," the pastor said.

I stood up and moved to the center of the circle of chairs filled with about a dozen participants. With my eyes closed I didn't feel or "see" a thing.

"I'm not getting anything," I said, feeling frustrated.

"See if something pops into your mind—maybe a musical instrument," she said encouragingly.

As soon as she said "musical instrument," I saw a drumstick in my mind's eye. The drumstick was twirling, the way it would if a drummer had flipped it up into the air. As I focused on it, it changed its form. It kept twirling and twirling, but now I could see that this wasn't a drumstick; it was a baton, the kind of thing a cheerleader might twirl and spin high into the air.

"I see a baton twirling around," I said. Then I saw a tall hat with a visor, like the kind West Point army cadets wear when they're on parade. The hat had a feather attached to the front, sticking up straight, with the top of the feather much higher than the top of the hat. It was white and shiny like plastic. In my mind's eye, I looked down towards my feet and saw a pair of shiny white shoes. Moving my mental sight up the legs I could see a white pair of pants with a dark stripe running up the outside pant leg. It was unmistakable—I was "seeing" a drum major.

"The guy is pumping the baton up and down like he's marching in a parade!" I exclaimed. Then I could "see" the drum major kicking his knees up very high. As he marched along—left, right, left, right—each knee kicked up so high it almost hit his chest. I found it difficult to find the words to describe what I was experiencing, so I impulsively decided it might be easier to just act it out.

"He's going like this..." I said, and with what must have looked like an absurd thing for a middle-aged man to be doing, I started marching around the circle mimicking the drum major's moves. I brought my knees up and down as high as I could, and I pumped my arm up and down as if waving a large baton.

Immediately, an elderly lady sitting to my left said, "He could go so high we thought he'd never come down."

"Do you know who this is?" I asked.

"Of course," she said. "It's the drum major from my high school marching band. It's funny, that's the first time he's ever come through."

Then another startling thing happened. As soon as the elderly lady made the connection to this spirit, my internal vision became an external vision. What I mean by that is I could still see the spirit when I opened my eyes. The vision moved from being confined to my mind's eye while I had my eyes closed, to taking place right in front of me with my normal vision. I was sure I could see the spirit move from where I was standing, and go to the front of the room, sit down, and point to something—I couldn't be sure whether it was his baton or a clarinet—at the elderly lady. I could also tell that he was laughing, having a grand old time, and delighted that he could renew the connection with his old classmate.

I attended the church and these Development Circle meetings for more than two years and had countless experiences of giving and receiving spirit messages. On occasion I gave messages from the platform, performing the clairvoyance and billet reading that takes place during the church service. Also, the pastor encouraged me to do two more things to help develop my psychic ability: I soon formed a monthly circle of friends who met in my home to practice mediumship, and I completed an intensive correspondence course of study—the Educational Course on Modern Spiritualism—through the Morris Pratt Institute in Milwaukee, Wisconsin.

PART II ADVENTURES WITH JOSHUA FROM THE SPIRIT WORLD

7 "HEARING" THE DEAD

One of the reasons I had become interested in developing my own spiritual senses was that I wanted to be able to communicate with my son Joshua directly without the need for a medium. If I could become a medium myself I could be sure that the messages I was getting from Josh were genuine, accurate, and not lost in the translation of the images or words received by some other medium.

Just as I had hoped, this is what eventually happened. One of the most exciting direct communications I received from Joshua happened on July 11, 2009. I had been adding a chapter entitled, "What Life is Like in 'Heaven'" to *Reconciled by the Light: the After-Death Letters from a Teen Suicide.* I was getting close to finishing the book, and I was experiencing the frustration of trying to find a publisher. In an earlier communication through a medium, I came to believe that Josh had said that there was a publisher that would take the book if I were patient enough and persevered to find one. This July 11 message had the effect of releasing me from the restriction that I had in my mind because of that belief. Here is the message as I received it early that morning in my bedroom:

I'm happy with what you've been writing. This is really important content. I've been with you, as you have sensed, because I'm excited about what you've been doing. Don't let my prediction of September (for publisher to appear) influence you. If you feel strongly to self-publish, go for it!

That was just one possibility out there, but nothing's etched in stone. Don't worry about the job situation and money. Just focus on what you feel needs to be done. I'm with you. You feel me right now (as you're writing this). There is a lot of support for this project in high places.

Also, it's okay to be patient. I know you're in a big hurry, but you needn't be.

In one sense, there's plenty of time. While on the other hand, I feel/know your sense of urgency, and that's not a bad thing.

Good luck.
Josh

This message was exciting to me on more than one level. First, this was a very powerful experience of another type of mediumship called *clairaudience*, which is French for "hearing clearly." Instead of receiving impressions of objects, symbols, or letters, it felt as if I was hearing words in my brain. Somehow I knew what Josh was trying to say to me. It came very fast, and I had to grab a pen and paper really quickly and write as fast as I could to get it down before I lost it.

I was ecstatic. Not just because I felt released from the obligation to use an established publisher to print the book, but I was also jumping for joy because this was a major breakthrough in my ability to communicate with Joshua.

I immediately got on the phone to Cherie Lassiter, a very gifted medium that works in the Raleigh area, and scheduled a reading with her for July 15. I thought that since this was the first time I had received such a detailed message from Joshua, I'd like to see if another medium would confirm it. Then I would know in an *evidentiary* way that it was actually Joshua that gave me my message and that I had received it accurately.

Four days later, I arrived at Cherie's apartment. We sat in a beautiful little garden she had outside her back door. I took out a tape recorder, but I couldn't get it to work. So instead I pulled out a legal pad and started to write down what she was receiving.

Fortunately, Joshua came through very easily and strongly.

With her eyes closed, Cherie heard Joshua say, "He's writing."

She opened her eyes and glanced over at me, scribbling away on my legal pad. "Oh, *you're* writing," she said. Then it seemed she realized Joshua wanted to talk about the book I was writing, not just what I was writing on the legal pad.

"You think that you wrote the book, but he's saying that *he* wrote the book through you." Cherie relayed the message that Joshua meant that he and I were working as partners toward a common goal, and that he would continue to be available to help me in my work.

Josh went on to encourage me to self-publish if that's what I wanted to do.

"If you do this, you'll be speaking in a few months, and eventually a publisher *will* pick the book up, but they'll want you to make some changes to it—maybe make it bigger," he said through Cherie.[v]

The prediction of speaking turned out to be correct, but the time period was wrong; it took more than a few months before my first booking. Public speaking has now become a second career for me, and it's all because I went ahead and self-published my book. I've been invited to speak at churches, universities, youth groups, and psychic organizations like the Rhine Research Center and Spiritual Frontiers Fellowship.

Public speaking led me to begin conducting workshops for others who wanted to develop their psychic faculties or just learn more about the spirit world and how spirit communication takes place. I also began offering professional psychic readings for people interested in getting personal messages from the other side.

This has become the most rewarding "job" I have ever had; I really don't consider it a job because I enjoy it so much I don't consider it work. I find the practice of helping people discover more about who they are, guiding them towards their own direct encounters with God, and connecting them to lost loved ones to be meaningful beyond measure. During the process of my work I am often moved to tears.

One huge side benefit to this work is that it has brought both Connie and me into closer and closer communication and partnership with Joshua. We have experiences with him on a regular basis. Many of them come with demonstrations of his unique sense of humor, and are often full of wild and unexpected details.

8 VISITATIONS FROM JOSHUA

One of the most interesting spiritual experiences I had with Joshua happened in February of 2012. I had been invited to give a Suicide Prevention talk at a church in Raleigh, recounting the experience of losing my son to suicide and sharing information about the steps that can be taken to prevent other suicides from taking place. The church was a fundamentalist Christian church, and had a very strict doctrine regarding life after death. In a nutshell, this church taught that when someone died, they were buried "six feet under" and would remain in a sleep state until the return of Jesus on Resurrection Day. Then the physical bodies of the dead would rise out of their graves and come back to life.

I was a little nervous about what might happen if the subject of spirit communication came up. The Suicide Prevention part of my program was well-received, and then came the question and answer session. That went well, too, until a woman asked me a question about handling grief.

"How did you deal with the sadness that came from losing your son?" she asked.

"Well," I answered, "I believe in the gift of 'prophecy,' so I sought to get communication from my son after he died. By doing that, I was comforted by the knowledge that he was still around, and that he was OK."

That's all I said about spirit communication, but that was plenty. The pastor became very agitated, and after I fielded a couple more questions, he felt compelled to come up and try to undo the damage I had done to his dogma.

He took the microphone from me and reminded the congregation that dead people were sleeping in their graves, so that it wasn't possible to get messages from them. He also warned them, with particular emphasis to the young people, that Satan was a tricky fellow, and they would be wise to stay to the tried and true path of fundamentalist Christianity.

To my surprise, he wasn't even happy with my suggestion that the best way to avoid suicidal thinking was to make a strong personal relationship with God. I told the young people in particular that it was okay to say anything to God in prayer—to be honest about their feelings with him even if they were angry or upset.

I had said, "Prayer should be like a baby crying for its mother's milk."

The pastor didn't like that either.

Connie and I were sitting right in front of him in the first pew. While I found it amusing to watch the pastor flailing around spewing fear of damnation, I was really saddened by the thought that this fearfulness might wind up blocking people from opening their hearts to a direct experience with God. In my view, if our basic conception of God is that he is an angry sovereign ready to punish us miserable sinners any time we get out of line, this can block us from a genuine experience of God's unconditional love.

It has been my experience, confirmed by numerous mystical experiences, that God is a loving parent, eager to communicate *that* to us and honestly not very interested in judgment and "Hell-fire."

So it was with a feeling of disappointment that Connie and I left the church and climbed into our trusty Dodge van for the trip home. Driving down the interstate, I commented to Connie how sad it was that some members of the church were so closed to receiving any new information that might contradict their doctrine.

Immediately, I saw Joshua through *clairvoyance*. He was sitting in the back seat, head tilted down slightly, and shaking it back and forth. Through *clairaudience*, I heard him say "Those people, those people!" with an air of not exactly frustration in his voice, but more like bemusement and sadness at their narrow-mindedness.

Connie said, "Joshua's in the back seat."

"You see him, too?" I asked.

"Yeah," she replied. "He's shaking his head, 'No.'"

I was astonished. "I saw him shaking his head back and forth, too, but I heard him saying 'Those people, those people.' I think he's disappointed that they weren't more open-minded."

"Yeah, I think so, too," she said.

We were both amazed. While both Connie and I have had numerous spiritual encounters with Joshua, that was the first time we both perceived his presence and location *at the same time*.

After I spoke and did platform readings at a Spiritual Frontiers Fellowship program, Connie and I conducted a workshop at my home for several people who wanted to know more about

24

spirit communication, develop their own psychic abilities, and receive readings from me.

The day before the workshop, we prepared the family room to receive the participants. It's a large room with a fireplace in the front, and over the fireplace was a picture of the signing of the United States Constitution. It had been hanging there undisturbed for more than twenty years. On that day, when I looked at the picture, I was surprised to see that somehow the print had become separated from the matting and was hanging crooked inside the frame.

"I wonder how that happened," I said to Connie. "No problem. I can probably fix that in no time."

I took the picture down, thinking I could pop the frame right open and reattach the print with a piece of Scotch tape, but then I saw that the backing had been thoroughly sealed on all four sides with packaging tape.

"Man! We don't have time to fix this right now. I'm just going to put it in my office for later," I said, and carried the picture over to the adjoining room. "Do we have another picture we can hang there in its place?" I asked, looking around in my office.

"I don't know," said Connie.

"Oh well," I replied. "We'll think of something later."

The missing picture left a big empty space right in the center of the room, where everybody's eyes would be facing during the workshop.

"Boy, that sure doesn't look right," I thought.

In the afternoon, I lay down to take a nap, and while I was half-asleep, Joshua appeared to me. He only showed me his face, but, oddly enough, he showed it in profile. I didn't mind at all because I could see all the details of the side of his face—his cheek with the peach-fuzz on it, his ear, and the way his hair curled over it. I was so happy to see his beautiful face. Then he showed me his entire body. He was standing, facing the fireplace with his right arm extended, pointing at the empty space above the mantel where the picture had been. I didn't hear any words, but nevertheless I could sense that he wanted us to hang a picture of him in that space.

I got up, found Connie, and told her what had happened.

"What picture of Josh can we hang there?" I asked her.

"What about his high school portrait hanging in the dining room," she replied.

"I don't like that picture," I said. "His eyes look weird to me in that one."

There was a moment of silence as we racked our brains.

"Hey, wait a minute!" I exclaimed. "What about that other one in the bedroom?"

I sprinted up the stairs and grabbed a really beautiful photo that we had liked so much that we had it enlarged and framed. As I brought it down to show Connie I noticed something that confirmed the spiritual vision of Joshua: the photo was of his face only, in *profile.*

I think that the reason Joshua wanted that photo hanging in the workshop space was that it created some type of connecting point or portal for him to more easily participate in the workshop. Now I always have a picture of him hanging during workshops and when I give readings.

We held our first workshop the next day, and during the lunch break, a few of the participants wandered outside on our back deck. Although I didn't know it at the time, one of the ladies who went out there was already a very gifted medium. Her name is Alma Palmer, and she is a professional medium in the Raleigh, North Carolina area. When we gathered back to begin the second part of the workshop, Alma raised her hand.

"Yes," I said.

"I received a message during lunch, and I'm supposed to share it with the whole group," she said.

"Go right ahead," I said, intrigued.

"When I was out on the deck, Joshua came to me," Alma said. "He asked me 'Are you enjoying the workshop?' I said 'Yes.' Then he said 'My dad's pretty awesome, isn't he?' and I said 'Yes.' So he just wants everybody to know that he's very involved with what's going on here today."

That's the way it's been ever since. In every workshop we've had, at least one person has had a direct encounter with Joshua.

9 Joshua communicating through the First Book—*Reconciled by the Light: the After-Death Letters from a Teen Suicide*

A few months later, in December of 2011, we held another mediumship workshop in Clayton, North Carolina. A couple of women who ran a business invited Connie and me to conduct a couple of workshops at their office. We held an introductory workshop first, and an advanced workshop a few weeks later. When we arrived for the advanced workshop, we were surprised to find that one of the participants was a sixteen-year-old girl. Her mother had signed up for the workshop, but for some reason couldn't make it, so the daughter asked if she could take her mom's place. I was a little hesitant because this was an advanced workshop, and the young lady – let's call her Kristen – hadn't taken the introductory workshop like her mom had. I decided to let her attend anyway, because she had at least read *Reconciled by the Light: the After-Death Letters from a Teen Suicide* as preparation—twice!

This young lady had already been having spiritual experiences, and she made an immediate heart-to-heart connection with Josh. This is not an isolated phenomenon. Connie and I have received numerous emails and letters from people who have also had some type of spiritual experience in connection with reading the book. Kristen explained that she has communicated directly with Josh on more than one occasion.

"He told me I can talk to him anytime I want to and he'll be there for me," she said. "He said 'Just don't *pray* to me.'" Hearing that Josh discouraged Kristen from making him an object of worship, I was very impressed with him. I believe he demonstrated the proper attitude of humility a spiritual teacher should exemplify. Kristen said that Joshua had helped her enormously in dealing with her own self-destructive impulses and negative thinking, and she was very grateful to him for that.

During the message portion of each advanced workshop, I guide each person, one by one, to perform mediumship themselves, if they want to give it a try. When it was Kristen's turn, I was amazed at what a powerful psychic ability she was already demonstrating at age sixteen.

After Kristen's turn, Connie spoke up to say that Joshua was present. She said that Josh told her "I've got this one," referring to Kristen. Connie could see that there was a strong spiritual connection between Kristen and Josh, and that Josh was empowered to provide some type of protective energy around Kristen. Connie felt that we were supposed to tell Kristen's parents that she was now out of danger of self-destruction, and would be fine from now on. Connie and I had seen this type of thing before. Readers of the first volume of *Reconciled by the Light* will remember that Joshua said he is part of a "Task Force" made up of many other spirits who work on the earth plane to help prevent suicide and heal mental illnesses. I thought that when Josh said, "I've got this one," he was really meaning "*We've* got this one."

After Kristen completed the advanced workshop, she began attending the monthly Spirit Circle that Connie and I host at our home. I felt on those occasions that she needed to attend the introductory workshop. I didn't mind that she got the order backwards, it was just that there was material in the introductory workshop that I thought was very important for her to know.

I finally got her to attend a workshop after giving her a big discount in light of the fact that her only income came from babysitting whenever the opportunity presented itself.

Apart from providing people with an understanding of what spirit communication is and how it takes place, I have a couple of higher goals for these workshops:

First, it is to help people uncover a clearer picture of who they are and what their value is. This centers around the idea that each human being is a precious child of God, an actual expression of God's character in human form—the "image and likeness" of God.[vi] In my view, the most important thing is to *understand* that each of us is deserving of receiving the unconditional love of God—that this is our birthright as children of our Divine Parent.

Second, on the foundation of this understanding, the workshop is designed to facilitate a direct personal *experience* of the *love of God.* I long for people to have a similar experience to the one Jesus had at the Jordan River. While undergoing a baptism ceremony performed by John the Baptist, Jesus saw the Heavens open up. The

Spirit of God descended in the form of a dove, and through *clairaudience* he heard God say to him, *"You are my Beloved Son; with you I am well pleased."*[vii]

Kristen had no idea, but she was about to receive both the understanding *and* the experience. I had no idea, but I was also about to have a spiritual experience of a type I had never experienced before.

10 Joshua Introduces a "Friend"

During my workshops, I lead people through guided meditations in which many participants have reported having powerful direct personal spiritual experiences. I call one of these exercises the "Sun Meditation." One thing I like about this meditation is that it's really easy to do. Even beginners can have great experiences with it.

All participants have to do is sit in a comfortable chair—even a recliner will do. Then I play a recording of ocean waves on a beach. After they take a few deep relaxing breaths while listening to the sound of the waves, I ask them to just imagine that they are sitting in a chair on the beach: toes in the sand, soaking up the warm sunshine, feeling it on their skin. Then I guide them to a place that often leads to a mystical experience. Some report feeling a warm loving sensation coming from the sunlight, and some have encounters with deceased loved ones or other spirits.

When I led the meditation at the workshop Kristen attended, I did it a little differently than I had done it before. Some earlier participants had requested a recording of the meditation that they could download for use at home, so I had produced a professional recording of my voice with the sound of the waves in the background and loaded it onto my website. [viii]

This produced an unexpected opportunity for me. Because I had the recording, all I had to do was click the button on my computer to guide the meditation, leaving me free to do the meditation along with the other participants.

As I began the meditation, I relaxed into my chair and began drifting into the state that allows me to open up psychically. After a while, I opened up my eyes for a moment to look and see how the other participants were doing. As I looked around, I "saw" something I had never seen before. In front of the faces of some of the participants, I saw what looked like little tornados—rotating vortexes of spiritual energy. They weren't vertical—starting at the floor and going up—they were sideways. The narrow, beginning part of the tornado appeared straight out in front of each person at about a four feet distance, and then got wider and wider until the wide end was right in front of their foreheads. Each tornado started above them, like it was dropping out of the heavens, maybe about a foot higher than their heads, and gently swooped down at about a twenty degree angle, getting wider and wider until the opening part in front of their faces was about eight inches in diameter. The vortexes were shaped like angel trumpets, with the narrow end out front and the wide bell-shaped part right in front of the face.

In front of two participants, there were no little tornados. I could tell that what this meant was that those two participants had not connected to spirit. The others *had* connected and were having some type of mystical experience.

Like me, Kristen was sitting all the way in the back, off to my right. When I looked over at her, I was taken aback. In front of her face there was also a rotating vortex, but it wasn't the size of a trumpet: it was the size of a tuba! This thing was so huge it was as if she was completely immersed in spiritual energy. I knew that something amazing was going on with her, and I was dying to know what it was.

When the mediation finished, I stood up and returned to the front of the room.

"I could tell that you guys had some kind of spiritual experience," I said gesturing to the ones I saw the little tornados in front of, "and Kristen, you had a lot of stuff going on, didn't you?"

All Kristen could do was nod her head. I could see that her face was drenched in tears. She was still gently sobbing.

I asked each person if they wanted to share what had happened to them during the meditation. Just as my vision had indicated, the two participants that didn't have the vortexes in front of their faces said that while they enjoyed the meditation because it made them feel relaxed, they didn't have any experience out of the ordinary. One of them said her mind kept wandering, thinking about other things and distracting her from getting deeper into the meditation. This is a common challenge for beginners.

The ones that had the little tornados in front of them did have spiritual experiences. One woman choked up as she described a visitation she had received from her deceased husband. Another had a deep realization about a particular question she had regarding her spiritual life path. I honestly can't remember what the others said.

Finally, I asked Kristen if she would like to share something. She was still crying a little bit, even though a few minutes had passed since the meditation ended. I'm so grateful for her willingness to share her experience because I think it can be beneficial to a lot of people.

"After I got relaxed into my chair on the beach, I looked down the beach to my left, and I saw Joshua down there," Kristen said. "So I jumped out of my chair, ran down the beach as fast as I could, and tackle-hugged him. It was so great to feel his embrace. I just stayed there and talked with him. I told him how grateful I was to him for being my friend and for all he had done to help me.

"He just held me for a moment and then he spoke to me. He told me 'Actually, Kristen, you really shouldn't be thanking me. There's someone else who is really the one who helped you the most, and I'd like to introduce you to him.' Then he pointed to his left. When I looked over there, there was this bright white light. It was coming from the person standing next to Josh. As I looked to see who it was, I knew right away that it was God.

"I felt kind of nervous—I mean this was God! So I told him I was sorry—sorry because I felt I had been kind of ignoring him, and didn't have a very good relationship with him.

"Then he said 'No, I'm sorry. I'm sorry that you have had such a difficult childhood. I'm sorry for what you have had to go through; it was never my intention that it should be like that.' Then he just hugged me, and I really started to cry then. I could actually feel him holding me. The feeling is just impossible to describe. I felt so accepted and loved—so loved! I didn't want it to end.

"Then he said, 'I've placed certain people in your life to help you. Joshua is one of them, but there are others on earth also. They are there just for you, because I love you so much! I am here for you also, whenever you call out for me! I also want to encourage you. You have so much love inside your heart, I hope you will share it with others—give it out. If you do this, it will be very good for you.'"

Kristen was crying again, the tears streaming down her cheeks. I was so moved, and so grateful, that she could have such a priceless experience.

"Welcome home!" I said. "I really believe that this experience you just had is what it truly means to be 'born again.' I think today is your spiritual birthday!"

A few weeks later, Kristen came to my Spirit Circle and I asked her if anything had changed in her life as a result of the experience she had had during the meditation.

"Oh, yeah," she said. "Lots!"

"Can you give me an example?"

"Well, in the past, if I saw some geeky boy wearing a ridiculous shirt to school I might say something snarky or sarcastic to him. I *never* do that anymore. I'm a lot kinder and patient with people now."

That short comment spoke volumes to me. It demonstrates exactly the reason why I am so committed to doing anything I can to help every person have that direct, personal encounter with the Divine Parent. In my experience, whenever a person has the opportunity to taste the love of God, it is a life-transforming event, and the changes that result from it are positive ones.

I don't believe in apocalyptic transformations of the world. I don't think that the Kingdom of Heaven will arrive like a Hollywood film production with the clouds parting and miraculous signs and wonders happening all around.

I'm convinced it will be more like when Jesus said:

"The kingdom of God does not come with observation; nor will they say, 'See here!' or 'See there!' For indeed, the kingdom of God is within you." (Luke 17:20,21 NKJV)

When a person experiences God personally, his or her heart is moved, and when the heart is moved, the individual is transformed. Then, when we know how much we are valued and loved by God, we begin to see people in a different light.

We gain a strong sense that if we are loved and precious to God, then everyone else is as well. Because we all have God as our Heavenly Parent, by definition we are all brothers and sisters— equally precious and loved—and we inherit a natural inclination to treat each other accordingly.

In my view, the Kingdom of God is the place where God is King, and that place is meant to be the human heart. If God becomes the King of each person's heart, then one by one by one, in a very quiet way, the Kingdom of Heaven will appear on earth.

* * *

Another example of Joshua's influence involves the case of a twelve-year-old girl. Her behavior had become so self-destructive that she had been forcibly confined to a psychiatric hospital. Her mother approached me for assistance one Easter Sunday, so we visited her at the hospital after church. I had suggested to the mother that she read my book right away, and if she felt it would be appropriate, she could pass it on to her daughter.

When we got to the hospital, I spoke to the girl from my heart, and she was very open and receptive. The topic of the book came up, and the girl said she wanted to read it—now!

"You want to read it before me?" asked the girl's mom.

"Yes," she replied.

"I guess she knows what she needs!" I said.

I went out to the hospital parking lot and got a copy of the book from my car. I came back and gave it to the mother, but the daughter asked for it right away. As we continued our visit, the girl was flipping through the pages, looking at the pictures, and stealing glances at the words between breaks in the conversation.

"You're just waiting for us to leave so you can read the book, aren't you?" her mom asked.

"Yes," she said.

"Well, I guess I better get going then," I said with a smile. "I'm already late for my family's Easter dinner," I said.

When the girl read the book, she felt an instant connection to Joshua. She told me afterwards that she actually wrote him a letter. She somehow felt that even though he was "dead" he would still get her letter.

A few years have passed, and this girl has been doing well since then. As of this writing there have been no more serious problems, and she is thriving in high school. So there seems to be some therapeutic value in the book for those who are open to receiving it.

* * *

I'm not the only medium that Joshua works with. A medium friend of mine also uses *Reconciled by the Light* as a resource in her work. She was conducting a retreat in Maryland in June 2011, and while reading from the book, Joshua made his presence known.

Here's an excerpt from an email she sent me of her account of what happened:

> *On the last morning of the retreat, I was sharing the words of Josh to the group, and I had to stop and smile in the middle of the reading. He was right there next to me and he said, "Slow down. You are reading this too fast."*
>
> *I didn't think I was reading it fast, but he must have been concerned for people to feel his heart behind the words. It was quite sweet.*
>
> *I was not going to read the whole reading, but he urged me to continue to read even what you wrote following about how you felt as a father to Josh. He said, "read on..........this is important for someone here." When I finished, a young lady who had come from Toronto and is 26 years old, was crying. She said that part of the reading particularly spoke to her because here it was Father's Day and she had not even thought about her father. She said she realized how precious her father is and how she has never told him so. About Josh, she specifically said, "He spoke right to my heart."*

11 MY PARTNERSHIP WITH JOSHUA

In addition to working with me during the workshops, Joshua often drops in when I'm doing individual psychic readings. This is particularly true when I'm doing a reading involving a suicide.

For example, I did a reading for a gentleman whose teenage son had taken his life. I had been hesitant to do the reading, because it had been less than two weeks since the boy crossed over to the spirit world, and I thought it might be too early to get a hold of him. I expressed my reservation to the dad, but he wanted to go ahead and do the reading anyway.

When I began the reading, I immediately saw a basketball in front of me as if someone were holding it up right in my face.

"I'm being shown a basketball right away here," I said to the dad.

Then I was given a vision of a boy about twelve years old, playing with the basketball.

"Was your son fond of basketball?" I asked.

"Yes, he was," said the dad.

Then the vision expanded and I could see the dad come into the picture, playing basketball together with his son. They were on a driveway, and there was a hoop with a backboard attached to the front of the garage. I got the feeling that this was at the house where they had lived together. After I described all of these specific details, the father confirmed everything as correct. No matter how many readings I do, I'm still the one who, perhaps more than anyone else involved, gets blown away by how accurate the information can be.

The next thing I saw was some horsing around. As they continued playing basketball, I saw the father reach out his hand and place it on his son's head, messing up his hair.

"When you played basketball with your son, did you sometimes fool around with him, messing with his hair, for example?" I asked

"Yes, I did," said the dad, smiling.

"I can see you doing this. What your son is communicating to me is that those were very special times for him. When you played with him like that, it made him feel very close to you."

I watched the scene for a little while longer, but I didn't get any additional information.

"Do you have any specific question you want to ask your son, like what he was thinking or what was going on with him?" I asked.

"Not really," he replied.

"Well, let me see if I can get him to open up a bit more," I said.

Then the reading took an unexpected turn.

Immediately, Joshua appeared in front of me. He came in the role of a protector. Then he spoke directly to me.

"Dad," he began. "It's too early to go there. This boy is going to be okay. I'm taking care of him, and there are others here that are helping him, too. But it's too early to even consider exploring deeper issues. We just want to give him time to heal from what he's been through; we can deal with the other stuff later. You can go ahead and tell his dad that he's going to be fine and we're taking care of him, but that's all for now, okay?"

This is just one example of many regarding how Josh will take an active role during my readings. He does anything he can to facilitate communication, and help in any other way that he can. For his assistance, I am deeply grateful.

* * *

I did another reading for a college girl whose ex-boyfriend—we'll call him Franklin—had taken his life about three months before she contacted me. As I often do when clients live in a distant state, I did this reading by telephone. When she called to make the appointment I asked her what her motivation was for doing the reading.

"Well, I just want to see if he's okay," she said.

We set an appointment for a few days later, and I called her at the appointed hour. The reading went well. I received some messages from deceased relatives and got some profound spiritual guidance for the young lady, but fifty minutes into the reading, there was no sign of her ex-boyfriend. Then I did something unusual; in an attempt to obtain some comfort for this grieving girl, I spoke in my mind directly to the ex-boyfriend, hoping he might respond somehow.

"Franklin," I said in my mind. "Don't be a jerk! This is your ex-girlfriend, for crying out loud. Don't you have anything you want to say to her?"

Immediately, through *clairaudience*, I received just two words: "sorrow" and "sadness." I thought to myself, "Spirit is being redundant here; 'sorrow' and 'sadness' are the same thing."

I discovered later that this is not the case when I researched the origin of the word "sorrow." The words *sorrow* and *sorry* are closely related; the dictionary definitions of both words contain the word *regret* in them. So saying "I'm sorry" is another way of saying "I regret what I did," or, "I feel sorry for my actions."

Those of us who commune with the spirit world are often struck by the economy of language used by those who communicate with us from the other side. It takes effort and energy to produce these messages; they will often get their point across in as few words as possible. It reminds me of the days of telegrams—when keeping them as brief as possible was almost an art form because the person sending them often received a considerable price charge for each additional word which had to be manually typed out in Morse code.

"All I'm getting is two words: *sorrow* and *sadness*," I said to the girl.

Then I concentrated again to see if I could get anything else. Clear as a bell, I got this sentence:

"Everybody is angry with me!"

Franklin never showed himself to me or gave me any symbols or images. All I got was the two words and one sentence through clairaudience, but that was plenty. Immediately I sensed what was going on. I knew from what the girl had told me that his family *was* angry with him— they felt that he had brought shame to the family name, but I was pretty sure there was someone else who was angry with him as well.

The young lady had led me to believe that her motivation for getting in touch with Franklin was just to see if he was okay, but there was more to it than that.

"Young lady," I said. "Have *you* forgiven Franklin yet?"

There was a short silence on the other end of the telephone.

"Well," she said with hesitation. "Sometimes I'm still angry with him."

"That explains his reticence to come through and talk with you," I said. "You have to remember, he's really just a boy. He is already in a state of great emotional distress. If you were in his situation, would you want to talk to him if you weren't sure he would just yell at you?"

I could tell that my words really sank in with her; her heart was open and receptive. I spent the rest of the session giving her suggestions on how she could work through her anger and be of assistance to Franklin. I told her she could help him get beyond his sorrow and sadness and find release from his turmoil. When I explained to her how powerful thoughts and feelings can be in helping those in the spirit word, she expressed a willingness to do what she could to support Franklin. I suggested that she display one or several of her favorite pictures of him from happier times and interact with him with positive thoughts and feelings.

"You can say nice things to him through his picture. Pick it up and give him a kiss on the cheek. These positive vibrations can be of tremendous assistance to him on the other side," I said.

12 SURVIVING SUICIDE

I have some more advice for those who may have lost someone to suicide. Sometimes, survivors of suicide form an emotional attachment to the location of the suicidal event. This is understandable; that is the last place we associate with our loved one being alive. In many cases, it is an event or location that carries with it traumatic and disturbing images. I highly recommend letting go of these attachments if they are associated with traumatic and disturbing thoughts or memories.

I have a client who found himself replaying a "video" of his son's final act over and over in his mind like a movie. A few days later, he told me he thought he was slipping into depression and spending more time consuming alcohol than was healthy.

I told him that repeatedly going over in his mind the final self-destructive act of his son was a disservice both to himself and to his son. For one thing, I have never encountered someone in the spirit world who had committed suicide that wasn't profoundly regretful of the enormous emotional trauma their action had caused for those who were left behind. Without exception, these spirits view their suicide as a terrible mistake they wish they could undo. They certainly don't want to be reminded of it over and over again. There is a powerful emotional connection between ourselves and our loved ones in the spirit world; if we cannot get over the suicidal images associated with their passing, it makes it harder for them to get over the event as well.

If we think about the mistakes our children have made, and bring them up in conversation, how does it make them feel? Here are a couple of examples:

"I really love my son, but I can't get over the time he and I were staying at my best friend's house. My friend let my son and me sleep in his beautiful four-poster bed, while he slept on the sofa in the family room, and my son wet the bed!"

"I really love my son, but I can't get over the time he borrowed my sports car without asking me, and wound up backing into the neighbor's car coming out of the driveway!"

In my view, when we hold on to these feelings and past images it indicates that we still haven't fully forgiven our child.

Joshua also did a few things that caused a lot of anxiety for me and my family, but they honestly don't bother me any more. In these cases we need to find a way to forgive the child in order to heal the wounds. My mental technique is to think about what he needs now, in the spirit world. I'm sure Joshua doesn't need to feel the energy I would produce if I were holding a grudge against him over past mistakes.

Of course, letting go of these images is easier said than done. Here are some of the things that have worked for me. I have a "collection" of favorite memories I have of Joshua that bring me great joy, and I'm sure they bring him joy as well. One is a video of one of his early birthdays in which he kindly shares some food with Ashley, the neighbor's girl. He was so young – maybe three years old – that he couldn't even say her name correctly. As he presents the food to her, he says "Here, Asheree!"

Another is a memory of our time in Honduras together working on a service project. Teenagers from all over the world and local Hondurans had gathered in a small town in the hills outside of Tegucigalpa, working with pickaxes to break up the stony ground to lay the foundation for a cultural center. It was backbreaking work in the hot sun. I noticed one day that Josh kept working while the other American and European kids had taken a break. I asked him why he hadn't taken a break.

"Dad," he said with genuine sincerity, "these little Honduran teenagers didn't take a break either. They live off of rice and beans. How could I, a big, strong, well-fed American, take a break? It just didn't seem right." To experience the heart that he had for those less fortunate than he was one of the proudest moments of my life.

I confess that I have an unfair advantage over most grieving parents. Because I have an understanding of how the spirit world works, I don't associate Joshua's memory with the location of his death. I think about Joshua where he is now, vibrant with life in the spirit world. Of course, the fact that I encounter him regularly through spirit communication is an even bigger advantage.

Anyone can train himself or herself to think of their deceased loved ones as still living and active in spirit. Doing so heals the feeling of sadness that comes at the time of death. That feeling of sadness is caused in turn by a feeling of separation. Realizing that our loved ones are still alive in the spirit world, that it is possible to communicate with them, and that we will be reunited with them when we make our transition to spirit can heal that feeling of separation.

For married couples, I cannot emphasize enough how important it is for husband and wife to forgive each other if they experience the suicide of a child. If you can't find a way to forgive, your marriage probably will not survive. Studies I've seen show that anywhere between seventy-five per cent and ninety percent of couples divorce after the suicide of a child. It is tragic that couples will break up at a time when they need the support of one another more than ever. It will take a lot of humility and prayer to get through it. Counseling is helpful as well. Each partner will have to be willing to be open and listen to each other in a nonjudgmental way, with the determination to forgive each other.

13 HEALING FROM TRAUMATIC EXPERIENCES AND IMAGES—EMDR

Being the person to discover the dead body of a suicide can make one the recipient of some of the worst mental images a human being can ever experience. If we are unable to effectively process these experiences, they can lead to depression and/or the development of Post Traumatic Stress Disorder (PTSD). If someone is having difficulty dealing with the traumatic images associated with suicide – and they can be uniquely traumatic – there is a therapeutic technique that has been extraordinarily successful in healing the mental and physical distress often times associated with them.

The technique is called Eye Movement Desensitization and Reprocessing (EMDR). It was developed by Francine Shapiro, PhD, beginning in 1987. EMDR works by imitating the eye movements that take place while we sleep. At night, all of us go through periods of Rapid Eye Movement (REM) that take place while our brains are processing the information and experiences gained during that day's activities. EMDR reproduces this process in a therapist's office.

When we are exposed to a particularly traumatic image or experience, it is often too much for our system to handle. The experience is not always completely processed. In a sense we get "stuck" in time, and that experience or image can return uninvited over and over again. These intrusive thoughts can produce extreme mental—and sometimes even physical—distress.

Participating in EMDR therapy allows our brain to fully process the experience to relieve the distress. What happens in an EMDR session is actually quite simple. After doing an interview and assessing the situation, the therapist will invite the client to think about the image or experience that causes the distress. Once the client brings those ideas to the surface in their mind, the therapist will ask him to rank the emotional reaction it causes on a scale of 1 to 10—one would mean it doesn't bother the client at all, ten would mean the feeling is so intense it is almost unbearable.

While the client is holding the image in their mind's eye, the therapist will ask the client to open his eyes. Then the therapist will hold something up in front of the client's eyes, usually the therapist's fingers. Asking the client to follow his fingers, the therapist moves his fingers back and forth causing the client's eyes to recreate the same movements that take place during REM sleep. This goes on for less than a minute. Then the therapist asks the client to close his eyes, bring up the disturbing image again, and rank it again on the 1 to 10 scale. Amazingly, most clients will say something like this:

"Wow! Even though I still find the image troubling, my reaction to it is down to maybe a 7 instead of a 10."

Further sets of eye movements will reduce the distress even more. As simple as EMDR sounds, it has produced incredibly beneficial outcomes for countless people. It has the added benefit of working quickly. In many cases, a client can find relief in as little as three sessions, as opposed to the years that might be needed in traditional talk therapy. In addition to helping deal with the trauma of suicide, the United States Department of Defense endorses it for effective treatment of battlefield-related PTSD. I myself have experienced EMDR therapy, and the effects on me were nothing short of miraculous.[ix]

14 THE NEW FRONTIER—INDUCED AFTER-DEATH COMMUNICATION—IADC

Dr. Allan Botkin is a pioneer, a discoverer, and an explorer, but not in the traditional sense. His realm of exploration isn't the external world of mountains, jungles, or oceans, but the internal world of the human psyche. Nevertheless, in my view, his discoveries will have an effect on humanity no less significant than those of the great voyagers during the Age of Discovery.

Dr. Botkin is a long-time practitioner of the technique called Eye Movement Desensitization and Reprocessing (EMDR) that I wrote about in the previous chapter. It was while practicing EMDR that he stumbled onto a further extraordinary discovery.

He was working with a patient who was suffering from Post Traumatic Stress Disorder (PTSD), a condition experienced by many combat veterans. This veteran – Dr. Botkin calls him Sam – came to Dr. Botkin and told the story of one of the events that had helped trigger his disorder. Sam had been a soldier during the war in Vietnam. At his base camp, he had befriended a ten-year-old Vietnamese orphan girl named Le. Sam's affection for the girl grew to the point that he decided he would adopt this girl and bring her home to be his daughter in the United States after his tour of duty was completed.

One day, while Sam and other soldiers were loading a group of orphans including his future daughter onto a flatbed truck for evacuation, the enemy attacked. Afterwards, he found Le's lifeless body lying on the ground. The images from this experience were burned into his consciousness, often producing negative thoughts that wreaked havoc on his personal life.

Dr. Botkin and Sam agreed to try EMDR therapy. The doctor began the familiar technique of moving his fingers back and forth in front of Sam's eyes while the veteran brought up the old memory of what had happened in Vietnam. As it does in most cases, the EMDR technique produced the remarkable effect of desensitizing Sam from the traumatic emotions and physical symptoms he had been experiencing, reprocessing the experience into one that no longer triggers the intrusive thoughts and unwanted reactions.

As Sam's feelings of sadness decreased, Dr. Botkin performed one last set of eye movements, when something totally unexpected happened. After Dr. Botkin finished the last of set of eye movements, he saw Sam's face light up with joy. When the doctor asked him to describe what he just experienced, Sam said that he saw Le.

He didn't mean that he saw just the memory of how she looked on that day; he saw her as she looked now. She was a grown woman with long black hair, wearing a white gown, and bathed in a radiant light.

"She thanked me for taking care of her before she died. I said, 'I love you, Le,' and she said 'I love you too, Sam,' and she put her arms around me and embraced me. Then she faded away."

Absolutely convinced that he had just communicated directly with Le, Sam said, "I could actually feel her arms around me." He was in ecstasy.

At first, Dr. Botkin thought the veteran had hallucinated, but after similar experiences with several other patients, Dr. Botkin decided to experiment. Eventually, he moved beyond EMDR to a new approach he calls Induced After-Death Communication (IADC). He now spends a great deal of his time training other mental health professionals around the world how to practice this revolutionary technique.[x]

Dr. Botkin wisely takes a neutral stance on whether his clients are actually communicating with discarnate persons in the spirit world or experiencing something else that we just don't understand. In the final analysis, it doesn't really matter; if it is successful in healing people from PTSD and other illnesses, that's a good enough reason to practice it.

In my view, the results he has had with IADC are nothing short of a completely new type of spirit communication. Dr. Botkin has been successful in producing an IADC experience in the vast majority of cases. One of the reasons this is such a significant breakthrough is because he has discovered a way to put people into direct contact with spirit people without the need of someone like me—a medium.

When the average person has a reading with a medium, they can receive accurate and extraordinary information, but there is always the nagging doubt that maybe the medium got this

46

information not by communicating with spirit; maybe he just pulled it out of the minds of his clients through telepathy, or who knows how the medium got it?

With IADC, the client *is* the medium. It is a direct spiritual experience, which leaves no doubt in the mind of the client. The experience is so real and powerful, the client doesn't just *believe* they contacted someone in spirit, they *know* it.

15 *EVIDENTIARY* READINGS

I have spoken earlier about the term *evidentiary*. An evidentiary reading is simply one that provides proof that the message being given by the medium is from spirit. I define proof as information that any reasonable person would accept as confirming that the communication is coming from a discarnate source. However, the fact of the matter is, some people have such a skeptical mindset that no matter what spiritual phenomena they observe, they find a way to deny it or dismiss it.

One explanation given by skeptics is that while some of them can accept the existence of mental telepathy or extra-sensory perception (ESP), this does not prove the existence of spirit or spirit communication. For this type of skeptic, if I did a reading in which I told them their exact date of birth, gave the names of all four grandparents, described their childhood in detail, and described all the contents of their wallet or purse, they would still not be convinced I was in contact with the spirit world.

"You're pulling this information out of my brain; you're a mind reader, not a medium."

Spirit has a way of getting beyond that explanation, as these next stories about a couple of readings I conducted demonstrate. I don't know how a skeptic would explain these amazing experiences away, but I'm sure they'd come up with something.

Connie and I visited the Washington DC area in September 2011, on our way to a couple of speaking engagements at universities in Pennsylvania. We spent the night at the home of some old friends. They had arranged to have me give a little talk, sign some books, and do a few readings. After I spoke for a while and did a question and answer session, I went around the room and gave a short individual message from spirit to each guest.

When I got to one woman, Wendy Herstein, I could "see" a woman next to her that appeared to be Irish and resembled her very much.

"Do you have Irish ancestry?" I asked her.

"I don't think so," she said. "My people were mostly German."

"Well, I see an Irish lady standing next to you, and she looks a lot like you. You ought to check some old family photo albums and see what you might find," I said.

In November, we returned to the Washington area to do a one-day workshop. As I was standing at the front of the meeting room getting ready to start the program, a woman came walking up the center aisle towards me with great excitement. It was Wendy, the same woman I had given the reading to in September. In her hands she carried two photographs.

"I want to show you something," she said, beaming from ear to ear, and held up two photographs. One was in color; the other was black and white.

"The color photo is me," she said, "when I was in my twenties. The other one is my *Irish* great-grandmother, who was also in her twenties when it was taken."

When I compared the two photos, they seemed to be of the same person. The resemblance was remarkable. The only difference I could see was that the woman in the black and white photo was dressed in clothes from a much earlier time period—maybe a hundred years ago.

After the workshop, Wendy asked me to do a one-hour private reading for her. During that reading, a gentleman came through wearing blue jeans and projecting the aura of a blue-collar worker.

"I want to say he was a real 'salt of the earth' kind of guy, hard-working, responsible," I said to Wendy. "He's saying to me 'We just did our best. We worked hard to take care of the family.'"

Then the man showed me a jacket he was wearing. He was very proud of this jacket. It wasn't anything elegant. It was a worker's jacket, but it was special to him for some reason. Then he stuck out his arm and showed me the sleeve. There was some kind of cufflink or metal button on the sleeve and he was pointing to it and waving it around to get my attention.

I described what I was seeing to the woman, but she said it didn't make any sense to her.

"Well, he's really emphasizing this cufflink or button for some reason," I said.

We concluded the reading, and about a week later, I received the following email:

Dear Ron,

Something occurred from the readings you did at the workshop that was very beneficial to me. On my billet, I had written my mother's name, with a request that she say something I could pass on to my sister and brother. This was because I wanted something to help bring my sister and brother and me closer together.

So when you got in touch with a "working class man, the salt of the earth," I immediately thought of my grandfather from Denmark, who we all loved most. You said this man was sitting quietly in a chair, and he said, "We just did our best. We worked hard for our family," and tears came. You said this man was showing me his jacket sleeve with a cuff button, a working man's jacket.

I called my sister to tell her about the workshop and that Grampa had wanted to be in touch with us, and we talked. Then I said there's one thing I didn't understand, did she?—about the working man's sleeve and the cuff button.

My sister gasped. She said, "That wasn't Grampa. That was Luch's (her husband, now in spirit world) father. I always wished I could have know him. He died in 1948, the year I was born. They were Mexicans who came to America and lived in poverty. Luch's father was a soft- spoken, gentle, hard working, salt of the earth man who worked hard for his family. He had a new jacket that he was very proud of. One day he wore it to work at the mine. His cuff button caught in the machinery and pulled him into the machine and killed him."

Sharing this experience of contact with a spirit world ancestor brought my sister and me closer. So I saw how spirit world readings can help us in this life. I am very grateful for your work. Feel free to share this testimony if you like.

Thanks and best wishes,

Wendy Herstein

I'm relating these two particular messages—the one about the Irish great-grandmother and the other about Luch, the Mexican

"Grampa," – because they are excellent examples of *evidentiary* mediumship. The key point in both messages is that I could not have possibly been pulling this information out of Wendy's brain, because the information *wasn't there*!

It wasn't until *after* the readings that she discovered the photo that confirmed to her that she had an Irish great-grandmother who resembled her. Also, she couldn't make any sense of the jacket with the cuff button on it until *after* she shared the story with her sister.

I love it when spirits do this type of thing, and they seem to love doing it as well – whenever the opportunity arises. It's such a dramatic proof or confirmation of spirit communication when people are given information from spirit that they know nothing about, and then have it confirmed after the reading.

Another common theme in an *evidentiary* reading is that the deceased will often use the cause of their death as a way to confirm their identity to the client. There's no way I could have known who this man was or that he had died in a mine accident. By revealing the unique cause of his death, he let Wendy's sister know exactly who he was.

Another example of this phenomenon happened when I did a phone reading for a woman who had recently lost her father. After communicating with the father for a while, another person came through. He showed himself to be a young man, and the woman asked me if I could tell how he died. The young man then revealed the method of his passing, confirming his identity for her—I was immediately shown a car heading towards the young man.

"Was it some type of automobile accident?" I asked.

"You're very close," she replied. "He was riding a motorcycle when he got struck by a car."

16 THE VALUE OF MEDIUMSHIP

On some days, I find myself ambivalent about my practice of mediumship. Communicating with those in spirit is not something I can control. I'm totally dependent upon the assistance coming from my spirit guides in order for it to happen. Also, the person receiving the reading has an effect on the success or failure of the reading. If the person has the wrong sort of attitude going in to the reading, it can hinder the results.

So sometimes I think to myself, "What if I give a reading and don't get anything?" The funny thing is, that's never happened. The guides have always come through for me. Still, it's a part of the "worry-wart" side of my personality that I've never completely overcome my doubts.
What keeps me practicing is the immeasurable value it has for my clients.

I remember the first time I did an individual reading on the professional level. A couple of weeks later I ran into the client in a bookstore. I asked her if the reading had made a difference in her life. She hadn't said much at the time of the reading, so I was surprised by her answer.

"After the reading," she said, "I felt as if a hundred pounds had been lifted from my shoulders."

To have such a profound positive impact on someone's life makes it difficult for me to walk away from mediumship.

One reading in particular moved me so much that I still think about it often. The reading was with a Hispanic woman – let's call her Juanita – who had been raised by her grandmother. After her grandmother died Juanita was surprised that she never received any kind of communication from the other side pertaining to her grandmother. She never felt her grandmother's presence, and felt that maybe she no longer wanted to be a part of Juanita's life. She thought that maybe her grandmother was disappointed with her or angry with her because during her teenage years Juanita went through a rebellious phase.

As I began the reading, I sensed the presence of a woman. Through *clairaudience*, I received just one word—"Mija."

"Mija" is a Spanish term of affection. It's a shortened version of two words—"mi hija"—that in Spanish mean "my daughter."

This one word immediately caused the tears to flow in the Juanita's eyes. As it turned out, even though Juanita was raised by her grandmother, the relationship was in reality, a mother/daughter relationship. The nickname the grandmother used for Juanita was—"Mija."

The grandmother spoke extensively with a deep tenderness.

"How could you ever doubt my love for you," the grandmother said. "I have always loved you, I love you now, and I will always love you."

Through *clairsentience*, I could feel the emotion, the deep heart of love that the grandmother had for her "daughter." It was so powerful that I choked up and began to cry, sobbing as I conveyed further words of love, approval, and understanding from the grandmother. She talked about how much joy she received watching Juanita raising her two young daughters. She mentioned that she herself had never known the love of parents, and that somehow she was being healed and comforted through the love Juanita was giving her daughters.

It was an overwhelming experience for both Juanita and myself. She left the reading feeling liberated and happy. A few weeks later she told me that the reading had somehow removed the block between her and her grandmother, and that she now often feels her presence. These types of experiences continually reinforce my belief in the deep value of what I am able to provide people.

Mediumship has value for several reasons. One of the most valuable services mediumship provides is comfort for bereaved individuals. I know from personal experience, having lost my own 17-year-old son, that the loss of a loved one is by far the most painful form of suffering most people will ever go through—at least it was for me.

In my view, the deep sadness that accompanies the loss of a loved one comes from the feeling of separation that follows the loss. If we can reduce the feeling of separation, we can reduce the sadness. Mediumship reduces the feeling of sadness first and foremost by providing evidence that the loved one is still "alive." Even though physical death brings an end to a person's presence on the earth plane, it does not bring an end to that person's existence.

The soul is eternal, and continues to live on in the spirit world. The soul retains all the memories, personality, and the love that it knew while it was in the physical body.

During a reading, the unique personality of the deceased person often comes through. One of the things that comforts me the most about communicating with my son Joshua is that his hilarious sense of humor is still intact, and he can still make me laugh even though he lives in the spirit world.

The second valuable service mediumship provides is proof of survival after death. Mediumship demonstrates that physical death is not the end of existence. Actually, there is no real death. What we call "death" is actually a "birth." It is a transition from one stage of life to another, just like the transition we went through when we left our mother's womb and entered physical life. As a result of the countless experiences I have had with the spirit world, I no longer fear physical death at all. To me, it is no more to be feared than the process of a caterpillar transforming into a butterfly. Leaving behind the empty shells of our bodies is like a caterpillar leaving behind its empty cocoon to emerge into a new life. Just as the life of a butterfly is a much wider and more vivid experience than that of the earthbound caterpillar, the life in the spirit world is a much more expansive and vivid experience than life on the earth plane.

Another way mediumship is valuable is that it provides an explanation of the purpose of life. Communicating with the spirit world soon makes it abundantly clear that the destiny we encounter in the *next* life is determined by how we conduct ourselves in *this* life. We learn that we are not simply the products of random evolution, but that behind the evolution is purpose provided by an intelligent and loving Being—a Divine parent who loves us as his/her own children, longs to have a closer and closer relationship with us as time goes by, and wants the highest good for us.

When someone encounters the reality of the spirit world— whether it is through a Near Death Experience, a personal encounter, or through the services of a medium—they often find that the things that matter to them the most in life get rearranged in terms of priority. The typical worldly struggles for material wealth, social status, and physical attractiveness begin to fade in importance. Maintaining loving relationships and helping others, improving our character and personality, and educating ourselves regarding truths of a higher order begin to take precedent.

It is appropriate to introduce here a related concept from Hinduism. Hinduism uses a term called *maya,* which loosely translated means "illusion." The illusion referred to is the perception that life is primarily material in essence. That perception causes many people to pursue wealth, status, pleasure, etc., at the expense of spiritual growth and development. George Harrison wrote a song called, "Beware of Darkness" in which he warns of the dangers of being seduced by this illusion.

Some people believe that the concept of *maya* means that the material world is literally an illusion, that physical reality doesn't really exist at all, but I think a little differently. In my view, the physical world does exist, it's just not that important. Spiritual life is what's most important because, after all, our physical lives are relatively short, while our spiritual lives are eternal.

I see the same point being made in Christianity as well. Jesus taught us to not make wealth in material goods our goal, but to "store up" treasures in the spirit world.

"Do not store up for yourselves treasures on earth, where moths and vermin destroy, and where thieves break in and steal. But store up for yourselves treasures in heaven, where moths and vermin do not destroy, and where thieves do not break in and steal." Matt 6:19-20 (NIV)

So how do we store up treasures in heaven?

I think the Dalai Lama put it very well when he said, "My religion is very simple. My religion is kindness." Practicing love towards all those we come into contact with creates spiritual wealth that will become apparent to us when we enter the spirit world.

One more point about the value of mediumship has to do with healing—healing of the heart. Spirit communication is an invaluable tool for bringing about reconciliation between those in spirit and those of us still on earth. Oftentimes there are feelings of guilt, regret, or a sense of unfinished business surrounding the departure of a family member or acquaintance. Mediumship provides a way to get closure, even if it's as simple as two people— one on earth, one in spirit—having the opportunity to say "I love you" to each other. In many cases the reconciliation and healing that takes place is quite profound and life transforming, as in the case of Juanita, the Hispanic woman I mentioned above.

PART III ADVENTURES IN EXPERIENCING GOD

17 WHY IT'S HARD TO "FIND" GOD

Having a direct experience with the love of God is the heart of the mystical tradition. It's very *simple* to do, but it isn't necessarily *easy* to do. That's because most of us possess "blocks" that prevent us from having the experience.

These blocks vary from person to person. Some of these blocks include feeling unworthy or unqualified to receive the love of God, being afraid of God, harboring resentment or anger towards God or others, and possessing belief systems that prevent us from being open to the possibility that we actually *can* have a direct experience of the love of God. I've had to overcome every block on this list and maybe a few others that I've forgotten about.

Trying to have a mystical experience with God reminds me of the story of Dorothy in the Wizard of Oz. It's a good illustration of the human situation. Dorothy's house crash lands in the Land of Oz after a tornado sucks it into the sky, but she wants to get back home to her family in Kansas. She is convinced that to do so she needs the assistance of the Wizard who lives in the Emerald City. She goes through a long, harrowing, life-risking ordeal on the way, battling different challenges until she gets to the city. Then the Wizard tells her she has to bring him the broomstick of the Wicked Witch before he will help her. She kills the evil witch and returns to the Wizard, believing that now he will help her. It turns out that the Wizard is a well-meaning but manipulative fraud, and although he tries, he fails to provide a passage home. When all seems lost and she despairs of ever finding her way back home, the Good Witch appears and tells her that she actually could have gone home at any time.

Interestingly, Dorothy asks the Good Witch why she didn't tell her in the beginning that she already possessed the power to go home. The good witch replies that *Dorothy wouldn't have believed her.* Then she tells Dorothy that all she has to do is click the heels of her Ruby Slippers and repeat a mantra—"There's no place like home, there's no place like home"—and she'll get home. She follows the Witch's guidance, and immediately returns home.

In this analogy, Dorothy is you and me, the Land of Oz represents our physical life here on earth, and getting back to Kansas means having that heart-to-heart mystical reunion with God—our true home. The Wizard represents certain types of organized/institutionalized religions, and the Good Witch is an angel, guide, or our higher self from the spirit world who is trying to tell us how powerful we are if we'll just get quiet and listen to the inner voice within us. She tells us we actually don't need to fulfill any preconditions, get anyone's permission, or obtain anyone's assistance to approach the dwelling place of God. We are free to do this at any time in our lives.

I can relate to Dorothy, because when I was young like her, I totally bought into a complicated theology and the institutions connected to it. When I was sixteen I got enough peeks behind the curtain to see that my own Wizard was no Wizard at all. My growing doubts caused me to become willing and open to explore beyond the confines of my particular belief system, Roman Catholicism, but not knowing that I possessed my own set of Ruby Slippers, I spent the four years until I was twenty like a pilgrim wandering in a spiritual desert desperately searching for the water of Truth.

I was a very devout religious child from the age of five, which is when I entered Catholic school. I memorized my prayers and attended church every Sunday. I was afraid to miss the Catholic Mass on Sunday because I was taught that it was a mortal sin. That means if I missed Mass on Sunday and died, I would go to Hell where I would burn in eternal fire and have a devil with a pitchfork continuously poking me in my buttocks. So from an early age I was taught to be afraid of God. Fearing God, it made me want to stay as far away from him as possible, so that nothing harmful would happen to me. I imagined I might get zapped by a bolt of lightning if I got him angry at me. So this fear-based belief system erected the first blocks in my heart to having a direct experience with the love of God. Even if God had arrived at the local shopping mall at Christmas time, sat in for Santa Claus and invited me to visit him, I would have run away instead. Still, hiding behind my Mom's skirt, I would have peeked out and tried to get a glimpse of his face.

As I got older, I did everything to try to appease this angry God, and yet, even though I was afraid of him, I was irresistibly attracted to him. Something deep inside me longed for a relationship with him. So beyond my attempts to appease him, I also tried to impress him. I wanted to get his attention without getting him too riled up.

For example, when I made my First Holy Communion at age seven, my Irish grandmother commented to me that she was moved by the serious and solemn expression I had on my face. I remember that when I received the communion host and returned to my pew, I prayed like a well-oiled machine. All you were required to say was a short prayer when you knelt down on the pew cushion, but I said that one just for starters. I had also memorized longer prayers called the Acts of Faith, Hope, and Charity—which is no small feat for a seven-year-old—and was confident God would be impressed with my devotion and sincerity.

Even though I was afraid of God, I really liked his son Jesus. He seemed to be a very nice guy. He liked kids. There was a painting in our school of a smiling Jesus hanging out with some kids. One of them was sitting on his knee. I wanted to be that kid.

In those early years of my Catholic upbringing, I never once had a direct encounter with God. In hindsight, I'm positive he was around and wanted to talk to me; he just had no opportunity to get through. When I prayed, I did all the talking. I never got quiet and listened to see if God had anything to say. Also, my prayers had been pre-written by church theologians. I memorized them and recited them back like a parrot.

I didn't think it was permitted for me to improvise a prayer—to just say what was really on my mind and heart—so I never did. Except once, and that's the day the miracle happened.

18 GOD ANSWERS MY PRAYER

I grew up in the 1960s in the suburbs of Los Angeles, California in a large Italian-Irish Catholic family. There were eight of us including my parents. My younger sister, Sabina, was prone to getting nosebleeds when she was a small child. Sometimes the blood would just seem to pour out of her nose, running down her mouth and chin and on to her clothes. My dad wasn't a person I ever saw get rattled, and he certainly wasn't one to panic at the sight of blood. He was a World War II combat veteran who had received two Purple Hearts for battlefield wounds. So whenever Sabina got a bloody nose, he would calmly apply pressure on the side of the nostril for a few minutes until the bleeding stopped.

One evening when I was about nine years old, she had a particularly severe nosebleed while the family was sitting around watching television in the living room. After a couple of unsuccessful attempts to stop the bleeding, my dad picked her up and carried her to her bedroom which was just a few steps down the hallway in our modest home. I could hear my parents muffled voices coming from the bedroom. It seemed they were in there for far too long. As the minutes ticked away, I could hear my father's voice getting more and more anxious.

Finally, in desperation, I heard him cry out to my mom, "I can't get the bleeding to stop!"

Now in every devout Catholic home there hangs a portrait called *The Sacred Heart of Jesus*. It's a copy of a painting that depicts Jesus from the waist up in a mystical manifestation. There is an aura of light surrounding his head, and in the center of his chest you can see his heart. It is bleeding because it is encircled by a crown of thorns, representing the suffering he endured at the time of his crucifixion, but the heart is also emitting rays of heavenly light representing his love.

We had a copy of this portrait hanging in our dining room. As soon as I heard my father cry out, I ran as fast as I could to the picture and knelt down with deep reverence. I bowed my head, folded my hands, and prayed like I had never prayed before.

The words were very simple. "Dear God, please stop my sister Sabina's nose from bleeding right now! Please don't let her die…"

I finished my prayer, and while I was still kneeling there I heard my father almost shout from my sister's bedroom with a surprised tone in his voice, "It's stopped! The bleeding's stopped!"

Strangely, I don't think I even mentioned the prayer to anybody afterwards, and I'm not exactly sure why. I was confused and couldn't accept the idea that I actually had the capability to facilitate a Divine act. I thought that it might be presumptuous of me to think that I had done so. Was it a miracle? I wasn't sure. Yes, I do believe now that the prayer created a condition for heaven to work, but I can't prove it. What I do know for sure is that this prayer was something very different and new for me.

It was completely different from all the countless Our Fathers and Hail Marys I had uttered. It was even a step up from my Holy Communion performance two years before.

It was different because of the state of my heart when I uttered it.

First of all, it was *my* prayer—it wasn't something I had memorized from a book. Second, it was *ardent*; it was full of intense feeling and passion. I put my whole heart into it. Third, it was *sincere*. I wasn't praying out of duty or routine. I was praying because I wanted to pray. Fourth, it was not self-centered. I *humbly* forgot myself and prayed for the sake of preserving my sister's life and protecting my parents from the sorrow they would surely have experienced if she had died. Finally, it was completely *honest* and clear. I told God exactly what I wanted, when I wanted it, why I wanted it, and I exposed my feelings completely without hiding anything.

It has been my experience since then that this type of prayer is extremely powerful. Just as I have always found the pull of God on my heart to be irresistible, I am convinced that God finds the vibration that is created by this type of prayer even more irresistible to him. He is drawn to a sincere heart like iron to a magnet.

Passion, Sincerity, Humility, and Honesty—these are powerful tools to have in your spiritual toolbox if you long to have a direct experience with God.

19 A QUIET PRESENCE

I didn't feel the presence of God that day, even though he may have performed a powerful act of healing on my sister. I didn't feel the presence of God for the rest of my years as a Catholic, although I experienced something vaguely mystical on some occasions.

Continuing my program of trying to impress God, I joined the church choir, and when I became old enough I volunteered to be an altar boy. As an altar boy I would be allowed to work with the priests and gain access to secret and holy places, which I hoped would provide me better opportunities to get on God's good side, and maybe start to develop a friendship with him.

I was particularly intrigued by one fact: the nuns had taught me that the large golden box in the center of the altar called the Tabernacle was "the place where Jesus lived." This box had a door on the front of it that was kept locked. The priest opened it during the Mass in order to take out the golden chalice that contained the sacred Communion hosts. They were composed of the body of Jesus—Jesus' actual flesh!

I figured in order to live inside his little Tabernacle apartment, Jesus probably shrank himself down to about six inches in height, just like Ant Man, a superhero that was part of Marvel comics' Avengers when I was a kid. At six inches, Jesus would have had enough room for a sofa, a fridge, and a miniature TV, so he'd have something to do while he was waiting for the priest to unlock the door to get his Communion hosts. I wondered if Jesus and the priest ever whispered messages to each other when the door opened.

"Good morning, Lord," the priest might say. "Thank you for today's Communion hosts."

"Your welcome, Father McLaughlin," Jesus might reply. "By the way, I put a few extras in there for you. Since the second graders have just made their First Holy Communion, you're going to need them."

"Thank you, Lord,"

"Blessings to you, Father."

After that exchange, the priest would take out the chalice with the hosts in it, and lock the door again.

Now nobody I knew had ever seen Jesus coming in and out of that door, and I was sure he didn't stay in there except on Sundays or for other Masses, so I figured there must have been another secret door on the back wall of his little apartment in the Tabernacle. In those days before Vatican II changed everything, the Altar and the Tabernacle were all the way back against the front wall of the church. Now that I was an altar boy, I might be able to find out what was on the other side of that wall, and who knows, maybe I could intercept Jesus and say "Hi" to him some day before he shrank down to go inside the Tabernacle.

The areas around and behind the altar were very mysterious. There was a Communion railing going all across the front, blocking anyone from going into the altar area. There were two recessed and hidden doors, one on the far left where the priest and altar boys entered a holy room called the sacristy, and one on the far right that was hardly ever used but led into a cloakroom where the vestments for the altar boys were stored.

The first time I was allowed into the sacristy, I was shown a narrow, dimly lit secret passageway behind the back wall of the altar. That passageway connected the sacristy to the altar boys' cloakroom. I figured there must be a secret doorway for Jesus somewhere on that wall, but I was never able to find it. However, there *was* a mysterious door on the far wall of the secret passageway. I was sure this had to be the door Jesus used to get into these back areas of the church.

I decided that when I had the opportunity and nobody was around I would go for it and open that door! I had never seen such an unusual door before. It was a normal door except for the fact that it had a pane of glass in the upper part of it. It was like a window, except that the glass had a textured surface and was obscure so that you couldn't see through it. All you could tell was that there was some light on the other side, but not like the light you would see if the door opened to let you out of the building. No, I was sure there had to be another secret passageway or room on the other side.

One day, I got my chance. I nervously approached the door and reached for the handle. It wasn't locked! My heart started to race as I began to turn it. Who knows, Jesus might be just relaxing in an armchair on the other side. This was the big moment. I opened the door, and on the other side I saw with utter disappointment—the empty fellowship hall.

The fellowship hall was just a big cafeteria with tables and chairs where everybody went for coffee and donuts after church. I would have to find another way to get a face-to-face encounter with God or his son.

I enjoyed being an altar boy. There was a mystical quality to it, although I didn't think about it much at the time. Sometimes I would have to wake up before the sun rose and walk the half-mile to the church for an early morning weekday Mass. It was dark and quiet as I walked to the church, it was quiet in the church, and if I got there before the priest, it was quiet in the sacristy. The only sound was a faint tick-tick-tick of the clock hanging on the wall. Oddly, there was a Presence in the quiet. I didn't feel alone or scared doing this routine, but it never crossed my mind that my experience was anything spiritual in nature.

Other things that nurtured the mystical seed growing inside me were things like the ching-ching sound the bells made when I rang them as the priest and I made our entrance into the sanctuary, the smoke and the delicious smell of the incense on Holy Days, the *Om*-like sounds of the Latin in words like *Sanctum* and *Oremus*, and the musical vibrations of the choir harmonizing sacred hymns. In hindsight, I believe that God was present in all these things, but I wasn't paying the right kind of attention. I didn't think to look for God in places like that. I was looking for God only with my head, and not with my heart.

20 THE WIZARDS HAVE NO ANSWERS

As I entered my teens, I really began to struggle with my Catholic faith. As a young child, I had been impressed by the love I felt from some of the nuns and lay teachers, and the pictures of Jesus as a boy my age helping his dad in his carpenter's shop enthralled me along with the whole idea of the Holy Family. I had comic books that idolized the works of the saints and the missionaries. I wanted to be a missionary, too. I imagined myself as a priest or brother in Africa, but I didn't want to just share the doctrine of Catholicism. I wanted to build dams and irrigation systems, so the natives could learn to farm using modern science and technology, satisfying their physical hunger in addition to the spiritual kind.

Now I was starting to question the whole program of my faith. There were two reasons for this. To begin with, as my intellect began to sharpen, I saw contradictions in the teachings. I struggled especially with the concept of exclusivity. Exclusivity is the teaching that one religion is the true religion, and all the other ones are—in a nutshell—deceptions of the Devil. According to my Catechism book, unless someone was baptized in the Holy Roman Catholic Church, they were destined for eternal damnation in the fires of Hell. By my calculations, when you eliminated all the Muslims, Hindus, Jews, Buddhists, Protestants, members of smaller religions, agnostics and atheists, and any Catholic who was in the state of mortal sin because they didn't attend Mass or had committed some other serious rule violation, it appeared that at least ninety percent of all human beings were destined for Hell. That seemed awfully inefficient for a God who was supposed to be Almighty and All Loving.

Secondly, my life of faith didn't feel right. That was the most troubling issue; something just didn't feel right. There was something lacking deep inside of me, and I didn't know what it was. My childhood faith was no longer enough to fill the need I had in my heart. I told my mom. She suggested I visit a priest in the parish in the next town, El Monte, to get some advice.

"He's real good with kids," she said. So I went to see him.

He was an okay guy, but he really didn't have much to say. He said, "Just keep going to Mass and receive the Sacraments, and everything's going to be okay."

So I did, but it wasn't.

The final straw came when I was sixteen. An Irish missionary priest had given a guest sermon during Lent, and after the Mass, he actually went to the back of the church and greeted the parishioners as they were leaving the service. This was something our parish priests never did. I got excited because I thought that I might get a chance to talk to him.

I always liked when the missionary priests visited. They seemed kinder and more approachable. They had been to places of extreme poverty and suffering, and seemed to have hearts that were more tender as a result.

I got in the back of the line. I wanted to be the last person he spoke to so I wouldn't have to worry about him cutting off our conversation to talk to anyone who might be in line behind me.

"Father, may I ask you a question?" I asked.

"Yes, my son, what is it?"

"Well, Father, isn't there more to being a Catholic than just going to Mass and receiving the Sacraments?"

Uh, oh! I don't know why, but this question must have really irritated the priest. He took his pipe out of his mouth and looked down at me intently.

"Now, look," he said. "We've been in this business of saving souls for two thousand years, and by God we know what we're doing!"

With that, he stuck his pipe back in his mouth and walked away from me.

I gave up. Somehow, I knew intuitively that this narrow belief system that *promised* to ensure an eternal place among God's elect when I died was actually a *block* to having a direct personal experience with God while I was still alive. I realized that if I were going to find what I was looking for, I would have to broaden my search beyond the boundaries of the Catholic faith.

21 SEARCHING FOR THE TRUTH

From the age of sixteen until I was twenty I was on a serious spiritual quest. I was reading like a maniac, and any time I stumbled upon a new religion I examined it carefully. In addition, I read the writings of people like Herman Hesse, Rene Descartes, Carlos Castaneda, Baba Ram Das, Alan Watts, and Robert Heinlein. I investigated Soka Gokkai Buddhism, the Hare Krishna movement, Scientology, and a meditation teacher named Roy Masters. I learned a great deal from each one of these various faith traditions. For one thing, I discovered that the religions of the world have many, many more commonalities than differences.

The most notable experience I had was with the Transcendental Meditation (TM) movement of Maharishi Mahesh Yogi, the Indian guru who was famous for having taught the Beatles. TM is a fairly simple meditation technique that makes use of a mantra, a sacred word you repeat over and over again that causes the brain and body to relax into the meditative state. It did exactly what it advertised; it calmed me down and released my stress—it even lowers high blood pressure if you have problems with that.

I'm guessing that Maharishi had at least one direct experience of the love of God during his life, because I discovered years later that he had created beautiful poetry and other writings that are usually produced only by great saints and sages who have had such a mystical experience:

The divinity of the Heaven dwells in our hearts as love. Love in the heart of man is the shrine of God on Earth. Blessed are those who carry the shrine of God in fullness of love in their hearts. — Maharishi Mahesh Yogi [xi]

Unfortunately, in order to spread his meditation technique as far as possible, his American followers packaged it in such a way as to be as inoffensive as possible to people of other faiths or no faith at all. So his representatives would say, "It's not a religion, it's a scientific technique."

Also, I never heard any of them use the term God when I spoke to them. The term used was "Creative Intelligence," which is an accurate term for one aspect of God's nature, but it's hard for me to imagine building a relationship of love or giving a hug to Creative Intelligence.

I practiced TM for about six months. Even though I enjoyed it, it had the ultimate effect of increasing the sense of longing I had for a direct relationship with God. I found the technique and the teachings rational but cold, impersonal, and analytical. My heart was aching for something more personal.

As time went on, I'm convinced those in the spirit world were taking notice of my intense longing for deeper understanding and communion with the Divine. I began having mystical dreams and visions that made me feel that I was getting closer to a spiritual breakthrough.

I was about twenty years old when in one of these dreams God appeared as a powerful beam of light. It was like the beam that comes from those searchlights you see at Hollywood movie openings or car dealerships advertising special events. Instead of starting at the ground and shooting up, this dream searchlight started in the heavens and swept back and forth across the sky looking down trying to find me. I had attracted the light by standing in my back yard, facing the sun as it set, and chanting "Father come, Father come…" over and over again with great intensity and longing. The more effort I put into the chanting, the more the beam of light responded to me, coming closer and closer. Finally, this powerful beam of light came right down upon me, and before it hit me, I turned my back and went down on one knee to protect myself from the impact. When it hit me, its energy surged through me like electricity. I thought this might be what it feels like to stick your finger in an electrical outlet; I felt the energy in my whole body. Oddly, it felt good and yet a little frightening at the same time. As the intense waves rolled over and through me, an idea popped into my mind: "I must see the face of God."

With all the strength I could muster, I began to slowly turn myself so that I could face directly into the light. It took a lot of effort to move, but I slowly rotated around until I was just about to look right up into the light beam—and then I woke up.

Well, at least I thought I woke up. The light and the whole scene disappeared, and now I saw the view from where I was laying in my bed, looking around my room. I lifted the covers to get up, and gasped when I saw that all over my sexual area there were ugly sores. Jumping out of bed, I ran to the bathroom with alarm.

I woke up again—this time for real—and when I checked my privates, everything was back to normal. Whew!

I was somewhat confused by this dream. Even today, I'm not totally sure what this dream meant. I have no doubt that it was a direct encounter with God, but it felt incomplete. I was really disappointed that I "woke up" just as I was about to look directly at God. My best guess is that I activated blocks that stopped me from having the complete Divine experience. These blocks may have manifested because I possessed belief systems that prevented me from accepting that it was possible to meet God, and that convinced me that I was unworthy of having such an experience even if it were possible.

Having received orthodox Catholic indoctrination for most of my life, I had been convinced that sex before marriage was a mortal sin. At the time of this dream, I had been in a long-term relationship with a girlfriend that included premarital sex. Even though I was no longer practicing Catholicism, these beliefs were still a part of me at least on a subconscious level. I may have believed that being in the state of grave sin—sin can literally be defined as "separation from God"—made it difficult or impossible for me to be qualified and worthy to meet God. I was too "dirty," and would have to clean myself up first.

Interestingly, shortly after having this dream, I broke up with my girlfriend and began living a celibate life again. Was my subconscious mind telling me "Maybe if you start living in sexual purity, the next time God visits you, you'll be able to see his face?"

For whatever reason, breaking up with my girlfriend became a catalyst that precipitated even closer encounters with the Divine.

22 MAN'S EXTREMITY IS GOD'S OPPORTUNITY

I thought it would be easy to break up with my girlfriend, but afterwards I discovered it was more like going through withdrawal symptoms after deciding to break a drug addiction.

The evening of May 19, 1975 was the turning point. It hadn't been more than a few months since I had experienced the "Searchlight" dream, and it hadn't been all that long since I had broken up with my girlfriend.

I was still living with my parents and working at a machine shop that made airplane parts. I was consciously waiting to see what would happen next in my life. I knew I was now being spiritually guided, because I had recently made a pilgrimage to a spiritual commune called "The Farm" in Tennessee, and over and over during that trip I kept meeting people and having experiences that convinced me I was either being guided by unseen spiritual intelligences or being followed around by FBI agents who were arranging the most amazing series of "coincidences" as I traveled across the country and back to California.

Late that night, everyone had gone to sleep except me, and I was by myself in the living room. My mind was churning as it so often did.

"I'm twenty years old, and I still don't know what to do with my life. I still don't know what it's all about. I don't even really know who I am."

I started to become anxious, and didn't know what to do. Thankfully, I was what my children call a "straight edge" hippie—I didn't smoke pot, drink, or do drugs, and I was now celibate on top of that. If I hadn't been straight edge, I imagine I would have just gotten drunk or stoned to drown out the voice in my head. If I had done that, I would have missed the opportunity to communicate with God. I didn't have my girlfriend either. Whenever I had gotten like this in the past, I would call her up, and she would tell me to come over for homemade chocolate chip cookies and a glass of milk. That would always calm me down.

I thought about calling her up—we had parted as friends— but I told myself "No, you've got to be strong, and face this on your own." I struggled and struggled, trying to find answers or to get my brain to turn off, but I couldn't. I remember my hand trembling as it started to reach for the phone to call my ex-girlfriend. I fought the impulse a little longer, and then I gave in.

I dialed her apartment and listened to the phone ringing over and over. Finally, a voice said, "Hello." It wasn't my ex-girlfriend, however. It was her roommate.

"She's not here," she said. "She's gone away to the desert for the weekend with some guy."

Aaargh!!! Inside, I groaned in agony. I was stuck. Now, I had nowhere to turn. In desperation, I grabbed a spiral notebook and began to write a letter I didn't intend to send. Directed at my ex-girlfriend, I just needed to vent the feelings of frustration and sadness I was experiencing, missing her and upset that she was spending such an intimate time with someone other than me. After I got my feelings out, I turned to a fresh, clean page and surprised myself at what I wrote next.

"Dear God," I began, "I've been trying to find you now for six long years. Why do you make it so damn hard? Pinch me so I can wake up from this nightmare. Throw me a towel; where's the locker room?"

I poured my heart out for about a full page and a half, asking for God's help. I didn't think so at the time—I was just venting—but this was a powerful prayer! In fact, it was probably only the second real prayer I had ever made in my life, the first one being the "bloody nose" prayer for my sister when I was nine.

What mattered was that it was totally honest, sincere, and from the heart. In that sense, it was a perfect prayer.

It only took God three days to answer it.

23 GOD ANSWERS ANOTHER PRAYER

May 22, 1975 came on a Thursday that year. I was supposed to go to work that morning, but when I woke up I received an inspiration to go to Long Beach instead. I didn't even call my boss to say I wasn't coming in. I just got in my car and headed south on the San Gabriel River Freeway from my home in South El Monte.

In recent years, I had learned that it was wise to follow first thoughts. Those were the ones that came from intuition, and intuition is a major factor in the guidance that the spirit world tries to give us. Oftentimes we get a great idea, and then doubts set in and we talk ourselves out of it.

My first thought when I woke up that morning was to go to Long Beach, so off I went. I chose Long Beach as my destination because it was the location of the closest Coast Guard recruiting station. On my recent pilgrimage across the United States, I had visited Washington, D.C., where I had fallen in love with America. The words of Lincoln and Jefferson that I found etched in stone at their respective memorials had deeply moved me. I had decided I wanted to serve my country, but I didn't want to kill anybody in the process. Then I saw a poster for the Coast Guard and it read, "Help us SAVE lives."

So my purpose in going to Long Beach was to talk to a recruiter about signing up. Arriving in Long Beach, I parked my car on one side of a street, and noted to myself that it would have made more sense to park on the other side, and wondered what made me do that. I walked towards the main downtown street, and as I approached it I recognized that the Coast Guard recruiting office was on that street, a couple of blocks to my right. Just then, I got the idea to use the restroom. I didn't really need to go, but my mind told me that if I spent a couple of hours with the recruiter, I wouldn't want to have to interrupt things to go to the bathroom.

"There's probably a restroom right around the corner," I thought, and because I was on the wrong side of the street, I made a left even though my destination was two blocks to the right. I walked the whole block and couldn't find a restroom.

"I'll walk one more block; there's probably one just up ahead," I thought.

I wound up walking *nine city blocks* in the wrong direction trying to find a bathroom. In hindsight, I'm convinced I did so because I was being led by Spirit. Finally I came to a Buffums Department Store and thought, "There's gotta be a restroom in there."

I entered the store and found a directory sign that said there was a men's room on the third floor. I went up the escalator, took care of business, and came back into the store. At that moment, riding down the escalator, a strangely peaceful feeling came over me. I couldn't figure out why I felt such a sense of well-being. Maybe it was because it was such a beautiful California day outside, with a blue sky and a few white fluffy clouds, or maybe it was just because I wasn't working. For some reason, I just felt really good. I wandered aimlessly around the store for a couple of minutes, smiling at people and enjoying the experience.

As I exited the store, a mysterious young man was standing on the sidewalk, watching the people coming out of the door. I was sure he hadn't been there when I went in. In my coat pocket I had a copy of Hermann Hesse's *Glass Bead Game,* and he looked like a character right out of the book. Somehow I just knew I was supposed to talk to him. When I got close enough to him he surprised me when he said, "Excuse me, do you believe in God?"

Startled by the question, I reflected for a moment and said, "Actually, right now, I'm not sure whether or not I believe in God anymore."

I never made it to the Coast Guard recruiting station. I followed the young man to a house close by where I spent the next eight hours hearing a new spiritual teaching called the Divine Principle. It answered every question I had ever had about the Bible, Catholicism, religion, history, and then some. I felt like I had graduated from spiritual high school, and had just entered the college level course. I was completely and unexpectedly blown away.

A young man from Austria named Leo Mattern spent hours teaching me and patiently answering all my questions. He concluded by saying that between the years of 1917 and 1920 all of the conditions had been fulfilled for the Second Coming of Christ to take place, and then he just fell silent and looked at me.

"Are you telling me that the Messiah is on the earth right now?" I asked.

Leo coolly and matter of factly answered "Yes."

"What do you want me to do?" I said.

"Study the teachings further," he said. "There's a van leaving in a few hours for a three-day workshop at a retreat center in the San Bernardino Mountains, if you'd like to go."

"I'll be on that van," I said.

24 A DIRECT EXPERIENCE WITH THE LOVE OF GOD

I spent close to twenty years in the Divine Principle movement, and learned that it was possible for anyone to achieve spiritual maturity and experience direct oneness with God. I had several mystical experiences during that time, and a couple of them illustrate the overcoming of blocks.

The first one took place in 1976, which was America's 200th birthday, the bicentennial. To commemorate it, the movement decided to hold national God Bless America Festivals in New York City and Washington, DC to remind our nation of the importance faith in God played in the founding of America.

This, of course, was going to cost a lot, so we formed fundraising teams that fanned out across America to raise the money. I wound up in the suburbs of Memphis, Tennessee. Day after day we went door to door at strip malls and office complexes selling candy for the Festivals. It wasn't going as well as we had hoped.

One day, it rained and rained. By the time the sun went down, I was in bad shape. My feet were soaked, as was my upper torso, because the rain had penetrated my jacket. I was cold, and my muscles were starting to ache from that feeling they get after being cold and wet for hours. My only rain gear was a black plastic trash bag that I used primarily to keep my box of candy dry.

For the last run of the day, the team captain dropped me off on a highway dotted with old motels and gas stations. As I walked across the lawn in front of one motel, my feet made that "sploosh, sploosh," sound you hear when you think you're stepping on grass but you are really walking in a couple of inches of hidden water.

In this miserable tired state, I determined to keep going and I seemed to enter an altered state of consciousness where I went beyond the discomfort of my physical condition, and began to experience a more spiritual state. At that moment, I decided to pray.

"Heavenly Father," I said, "Don't worry about me. I'm going to be just fine. I'm going to keep going until I sell all this candy, so we can have a great God Bless America Festival in June!"

On the outside, I looked like the most miserable person, but on the inside, I was upbeat and determined.

Then, something really strange happened. Off in the distance to my left, from the other side of the highway, I felt like something was approaching. It was like the feeling you might have when you hear a very faint distant roll of thunder. It's miles away, you can't see anything, and yet you know a storm is coming.

As this feeling came closer, I sensed an energy building and coming right towards me. Now it felt like a giant tsunami was rising, coming closer and closer. Yet I felt no fear, only a sense of curiosity wondering, "What is this thing?" The unseen wave now rose above me and broke the way you see a wave crashing onto a beach. It poured itself all over me.

The "water" that broke over me was pure Divine Love, something I had never felt in my life before. It was a love that I had never known—unconditional, all embracing, and powerful. The feeling was so strong that I felt like it was too much. It was even more intense than the "Searchlight" dream I had the year before. On top of that, I was wide-awake as it was happening! I immediately burst into tears, but they were good tears, tears of reunion. I felt the power of God surrounding me, embracing me in a perfect love.

"Turn it down, Heavenly Father, turn it down," I prayed. I felt that the love was too much, and my heart might burst.

After about thirty seconds, the wave subsided. I wiped my tears and continued my candy-selling mission, not sure of how to explain what had just happened.

At the appointed meeting place, the team captain, Tony Scazzero, showed up in the passenger van that was our "home away from home," but I was surprised to find it empty except for him. I had been the last person dropped off, so the van should have been filled with the five or six other members of the team.

As I climbed into the front passenger seat next to the captain, Tony turned to me and said, "Ron, I just want you to know that because everyone was having such a rough time, I decided to pick everybody up and take them out to a movie. When I got to your area, I couldn't find you, so we just went without you."

In another circumstance, I might have felt sad at being left out, but that thought didn't even cross my mind. Instead I actually felt sorry for my teammates. "Those poor guys," I thought, "they had to spend time in a theater watching some stupid movie while I was out having this amazing experience."

Something else went deep into my soul that was much more profound, and had a lasting impact on my life. It slowly dawned on me, that at the time the wave broke over me, I was the only person on the team, and maybe the only person in the Memphis area, that was voluntarily out in the miserable weather thinking about helping God. That realization penetrated my heart, and I couldn't deny the truth of it.

I felt that God was saying to me, "You've always defined yourself as some miserable sinner, undeserving of my love. Well, how about now? Can you continue to deny that you are indeed lovable, and deserving of my love? In your miserable state, you didn't complain, but instead tried to comfort me. You moved my heart! How could you not be deserving of my love?"

He had me. I had to surrender. His argument was too compelling, and the experience was too real. The inescapable truth was that God didn't view me as a miserable sinner, but as his child, who was deserving of his love. As a result, the block of feeling unworthy of God's love came tumbling down. The block existed because of the belief system I had embraced as a child. This experience changed my life, and made me feel closer to God than ever before. Four years later, I would have an even more direct and powerful experience than this one.

25 SHOWDOWN WITH GOD

This next experience knocked down the blocks of being fearful of and angry with God.

It was 1980, and I was working as a full time missionary in Rhode Island, something I'd been doing at various locations across the United States for the past five years. That summer, I noticed my energy level was dragging, and I was finding it harder to motivate myself to work. My intuition told me that while the weather was hot and my body was tired, the real issue was that there was a problem with my relationship with God. For some reason, I was still holding back, not fully committed to him.

I asked for and received permission to do a spiritual retreat, so I traveled to the small town of Accord, New York, to attend a workshop amidst the beauty of nature. When I arrived, I was greeted by a young woman named Annie Redmond who had been assigned to take care of me. I immediately felt a connection with her. I could sense the saintly heart she possessed and just knew I could trust her.

"Here's what I suggest you do, Ron," she said. "Go for a walk in the woods. Go as deep into the woods as you need to be sure that you have privacy. Then, just open your heart and talk to God. Lay *all* your cards on the table. I want you to tell him exactly how you feel, and tell him everything you feel, even the bad stuff. In fact, especially the bad stuff."

Annie seemed so confident and spoke with such care and compassion that I was sure she herself must have had a close relationship with God. Because of that, I was able to set my fear of God aside. It seemed that Annie had a special "hotline" to God. I imagined that as soon as I walked off into the woods, she would get on her "spiritual telephone" and tell God something like:

"I'm sending this young guy out to talk to you, and he's really struggling. Please go easy on him, okay?"

So I went with total trust in my heart.

After walking for a while I found a place where there was an ancient stone wall, and I sat on top of it. Then I started to pray. I searched my heart, trying to find what was bugging me. Then I said something I would have never dared to say if I hadn't known that Annie had my back.

"Heavenly Father," I said. "The way I see it, you are the one who is responsible for all the suffering of mankind."

I still wasn't sure whether or not a lightning bolt was going to come out of the sky and vaporize me for my impertinence. To my relief, nothing bad happened. Instead, I could strongly sense the presence of God there in the woods with me. This time it was more than just the powerful energy and unconditional love I had felt before. I actually recieved words! From some place deep inside my heart God opened a door. This time the experience was not from the outside in; it was from the inside out. I knew, clear as a bell, what he wanted to say. He said it without a shred of excuse making or defensiveness, and to my amazement, he said it with absolute humility.

"This is true," he said, "and I accept the responsibility for it."

I was taken aback by the selflessness of this answer. It wasn't what I was expecting. I had always imagined God as an imperious, majestic being, and to admit responsibility for a problem just didn't fit in with my conception of what his personality would be like. This was *not* the God I was taught about in Catechism class.

"You are cruel, uncaring, domineering," I continued.

"I am none of these things. Those who suffer bring it upon themselves. It is the only hope for them to change."

There wasn't a hint of judgment in this statement. He was just stating the fact, and there was a tinge of sadness in his "voice."

"What about those who are innocent, yet suffer?"

When I asked that question, God lost his composure. I was stunned to realize that just as I was being completely and painfully honest with him, he was being completely honest with me. Again, his humility and open heartedness just floored me.

He burst into tears and seemed to tremble from deep in his heart.

"Oh, I can't bear the pain! If a parent chooses to beat his child, I cannot stop it. Yet, even then, if that child could follow me, I could save him. I trust you, Ron Pappalardo. You can help my children. I can't, but you can! Oh, please, I beg you, won't you do it? (Strong tears)"

By the time he finished this part, I was crying, too. I felt like I was listening to a parent whose heart was aching for his children. I

79

was humbled by the sincerity and honesty of the expression. He was sharing with me as if I was a long time and trusted friend.

I felt bad for the other things I needed to say, but I knew it would be a mistake if I didn't get everything out.

"Forgive me, my Lord, but this also must be confronted: I have suffered, Father. I tried so hard to find you – to find the truth. From my infancy I tried. I have never been malicious, have I? I tried so hard, and I feel betrayed. Maybe this is blasphemy, but I really feel I need an apology from you. I need to know you won't take advantage of me. Why didn't you come to me when I was lonely?"

With great anguish he replied "You didn't cry out for me!"

When he said this, it rang true in my heart. Even though I had searched for God in books and exerted my reason until my brain hurt, I hadn't ever cried out directly to him until that night in May of 1975.

"I'm sorry, Father. I didn't know how."

"When you cried out for me, didn't I answer? Immediately, I answered. It was me, (In tears) you must believe me! It was me! It was me – no one else – who answered you! In three days I led you to my son." He was referring to the prayer letter I wrote to him that resulted in my meeting the young man outside the Buffums Department Store just three days later.

These words penetrated my heart, and I wept and wept. I felt such a genuine closeness and intimacy with this Being. I eventually stopped crying, and things were quiet for a while. I thought I was done. What more could I say to this? Nevertheless, the presence of God was still there with me in the woods. I could feel it palpably. He was still there, waiting for something, but I didn't know what to say. He helped me by breaking the silence.

"Something's still bothering you," he said. "It's okay. You can tell me."

Searching my heart, what I found in there surprised and disturbed me. Nevertheless, I just knew it had to be spoken. If I left it unsaid, it would have been like being dishonest, and I would miss this precious opportunity for healing.

"It's weird," I replied, "but I still feel like saying 'I hate you.'"

He wasn't surprised at all, or offended. His demeanor was one of absolutely gentle kindness, and I felt as if he smiled at me with tenderness.

"Ron, you don't hate me. You really don't. You just want to *know* if I *love* you." I'm not sure I got the next line clearly, and I'm not sure I understood it, but here it is: "In reality, I have felt your love for me."

"I was really lonely before, Father. It hurt so bad I wanted to die," I continued.

"If I hadn't allowed you to have that experience, where would you be now?" he replied.

I knew exactly what he meant by this. It was only when I had nowhere else to turn that I finally cried out to him, and that cry brought him to me.

"You've got a good point," I admitted.

"Do you think it was easy for me to watch you suffer? I only hoped it would be for a short time." I realized that God had been waiting and waiting for this meeting even more than I had, wondering how long it would take before I realized that I needed him this way.

"I can see now that it was out of your love for me."

"(Embracing me) I really love you, my son. You should know that. Don't worry about anything, just know I love you."

Even though he said this to me, there was still a remnant of doubt in my heart. I wanted even more validation.

"But why do you love me?"

"Why do you love (your ex-girlfriend)?"

"I don't know, because *she reminds me of me!*"

"There you go!"

"Wow, that makes sense."

When I said, "she reminds me of me," I had a realization. It dawned on me that God actually sees his own nature reflected back to him when he relates to us, the way a parent sees himself in his children. The Bible scripture that says we are "the image and likeness" of God took on deeper meaning to me as a result.

The last thing I asked him was about the tremendous fatigue I had been battling.

"Father, why is my body messed up?"

"My son, relax. Don't worry about it. Accept the reality of your limitation. Be calm when discussing it with (your superiors). ...Develop your Heart and relax. I can save the world through you *wherever* you are."

We paused for a moment, as I tried to take in all he was saying. Then he spoke again.

"Amazing how small your problems have become, isn't it?" he said with a smile.

By this time, I was feeling many different emotions— beloved, calm, peaceful, liberated, amazed, in love. Yes, I felt in love! I had been a devout Catholic, an altar boy, and a missionary for many years, but I had never felt anything like this before. This was the day I really fell in love with God. I've been in love ever since. I felt so accepted, so known and understood. There wasn't a single person on earth that I felt as close to as this unseen Father who spoke to me through a doorway in my own heart. Again, I thought we were done, but he had one more thing to say.

"By the way, I wish you would talk to me more often. Don't you think it's a good idea?"

"Yeah."

"Can you do it every morning and every night? I can really help you if you do."

"I'll try."

"Okay."

It was over. I just sat there for a moment, amazed at what had happened. Fortunately, I had brought my journal with me, and I had been writing everything almost word for word as it unfolded. The quoted text above is actually from that journal entry marked "July, 3 1980, 4 pm, Camp New Hope, Accord, New York."

I walked back from the woods in a state of intense excitement, energy, and inspiration that lasted for many days.

26 Visitation from the Divine Mother

I have had countless other mystical experiences with God and the spirit world since that day, but I want to recount just one more. This happened in March of 2011, after I had returned empty-handed from a convention of college student activities coordinators, trying to get bookings for the college speaking circuit.

Connie and I had borrowed the thousands of dollars it took to participate in the convention, and I had nothing to show for my efforts.

As I lay on the couch in the living room praying and meditating, I received a vision in my mind. I saw a small alpine lake, and a stream cascading down from the surrounding mountains. The lake was perfectly still, as calm as glass, and the stream's water flowed down a mountain and disappeared into the lake.

I asked God for an interpretation of the vision.

"The stream represents your efforts. Even though they disappear into the lake, nothing is lost. The stream is relentlessly filling the lake. Eventually the bank of this lake will burst, and a powerful work will pour forth from your efforts. Don't be discouraged! Nothing is lost."

After I received this message, I closed my eyes again and focused some more. I practiced one of the meditation techniques I use for connecting to the spirit world, and it led me to the place where I often see God. I was shown two chairs. On the one closest to me sat a woman; next to her on her right sat a man. I knew that the woman represented Heavenly Mother; the man represented Heavenly Father. Heavenly Mother did the talking.

"Ron, first I want you to know that even though you see two here, I am only one. I am only one. The reason I am manifesting to you as your Divine Mother is because it is most appropriate for me to come to you this way because of where you are right now in your spiritual growth."

She invited me to come and sit on her lap. I took the form and position of a child and did so.

"I want you to spend a lot of time right here during this period. I am healing you of certain wounds that you still possess from your childhood."

This mystical experience went on literally for hours. It seems silly now, but at the time I started getting worried because I had some important business to do at the Post Office. Heavenly Mother eventually told me "Go ahead and take care of your business, but as soon as you come back in the front door of the house, please come right back here to this sofa and we will pick up where we left off, okay?"

I did as she said, and when I got back, sure enough, her presence was still there, and the experience went on for hours more.

Interestingly, for about the next eight months, God only appeared to me as Heavenly Mother. After that time, the Heavenly Father manifestation returned, but God can appear to me as either the Heavenly Father or the Heavenly Mother. In my view, God is not exclusively masculine or feminine. God is the Source of both characteristics. Now when I pray, I address my prayers to "Heavenly Father/Mother, God."

27 God Makes an Effort to Help us Have a Mystical Experience

I certainly do not have a monopoly on mystical experiences. I've lost count of the number of people who have told me they have had at least one in their lifetime. In fact, I would bet that God has made effort to get through to every human being at some point in his or her life. I'm convinced that he certainly longs for every person to have a direct encounter with his love, and to have a relationship with them. He wants everyone to know they are loved, valued, and understood. He wants to be like a cheerleader or coach that encourages us to grow to our highest potential. I know from personal experience that at least in some cases he tries harder to reach us than we do to reach him.

For example, one time when I was deep in prayer I was shown a vision of a ladder going from earth up to heaven. There were ten rungs on this ladder. I was shown that the energy generated by my prayer only rose to the third rung. I saw God come down seven rungs to meet my energy level and connect to me. So he "traveled" more than twice as far to reach me as I did to reach him.

The way I understand it, the physical earth plane has a very low or dense frequency or vibration, while the various levels in the spirit world have higher vibrations. The vibrations are higher still the higher you go in the spirit world. To encounter the higher realms of the spirit world, it is a combination of our raising our vibration and the spirits there lowering their vibration until we meet somewhere in between. So it takes effort or energy investment on both our part and their part in order for significant communication to take place.

I hope these stories have been helpful. I thought it would be helpful to give a few examples of various mystical experiences, so you can have an idea of how to facilitate your own experience, and what you might expect to happen. These stories illustrate some of the various blocks that may appear along your path as you seek a deeper and deeper union with the Divine.

The bottom line is, God is even more committed to breaking through the blocks and embracing you in his love than you are. We just need to want the experience, and cry out for it with an honest and sincere heart.

I mentioned earlier the saying that, "Prayer should be like a baby crying for its mother's milk." One of my spiritual teachers mentioned this in a sermon.

When you think about a baby requesting milk, it's the opposite of politely trying to get the attention of a waiter in a restaurant.

Imagine a restaurant scenario—you want some milk, but the waiter is a few feet away. You stay in your seat and wait. Every once in a while you raise your hand and wave hoping to get his attention. Eventually, the waiter notices you, and walks over to your table. You calmly and courteously say, "Excuse me, Mr. Waiter. I know you're really busy right now, but if you get a chance, could you please bring me a glass of milk. Thank you so much."

Hopefully, a few minutes later the waiter reappears with your milk.

No. That is NOT what my teacher had in mind.

When a baby wants its mother's milk, it takes a deep breath and screams—"WAAAAA!!!!!" —at the top of its lungs. Its little arms and hands wave around trembling, and its feet kick in the air. It puts all of its energy into crying out, as if to say—"I'm dying here. I don't care what you're doing, I want you to drop everything and meet my needs—NOW!"

Praying with that intensity creates the kind of power and energy that breaks through anything that might be keeping you from experiencing God. If you have trouble experiencing the presence of God, give it a try.

PART IV ADVENTURES IN MODERN SPIRITUALISM

28 UNDER THE SIGN OF THE SUNFLOWER

My experience with the Wimbledon Spiritualist Church and later the First United Metaphysical Chapel led me to discover that beyond just the practice of spirit communication, these churches were also the repository of a set of ideas called Modern Spiritualism. These teachings had a powerful affect on me when I studied them. As I mentioned earlier, discovering the Divine Principle movement after having been a Catholic for twenty years had made me feel like I had graduated from spiritual high school and entered the college level course of study. Discovering Modern Spiritualism made me feel like I had left college for graduate school.

I dove into the study of Spiritualism with excitement, and there were days when I felt that I must have been walking around with my jaw open in astonishment over the things I was learning. It was an absolutely mind-blowing experience.

A comprehensive exposition of what I learned will perhaps be contained in a future book, but I want to touch upon a few key ideas here. The term Modern Spiritualism is used to distinguish the Modern movement from older forms of spiritualism. (For the sake of brevity I will use the term Spiritualism instead of Modern Spiritualism in most cases.) Spiritualism has its roots in Shamanism, which is perhaps the most ancient of religions, practiced since prehistoric times. Throughout human history, there have always been individuals who have had the ability to communicate with the spirit world. Different cultures have given them different names—shaman, prophet, oracle, medicine man, witch doctor, mystic. The list is endless, but they are all practicing the same thing: mediumship.

Modern Spiritualism traces its origin to a cottage in the small settlement of Hydesville, near the city of Rochester, New York. Mr. and Mrs. John Fox and their two daughters Margharetta and Catherine (Kate) moved into the cottage in 1847, and began experiencing poltergeist activity in the form of rapping sounds on doors and walls, the moving of furniture, and the sound of footsteps walking through the hallway and down to the cellar. Mrs. Fox concluded that the house was haunted.

On the evening of March 31, 1848, a breakthrough occurred. Kate, who was eleven years old at the time, spoke to the unseen spirit in the presence of her mother and sister. She had given the spirit a nickname – Mr. Splitfoot.

"Mr. Splitfoot," she said, "Do as I do."

With that command, she clapped her hands a few times, and the spirit responded by making rapping noises on the wall—the exact same number of raps as Kate's hand claps. With that simple act, a code was established to allow for communication with the spirit world. The family asked the spirit to confirm letters of the alphabet by a certain number of rappings, and through this method, was told that the spirit's name was Charles B. Rosna. Through this spirit communication, Mr. Rosna testified that he had been a traveling peddler, was murdered in this house five years earlier, and was buried in the cellar. In 1904, a human skeleton was found buried in the cottage's cellar walls.

Later, at the Rochester home of another Fox sister, Leah, a message of a more profound and celestial nature was received through spirit rappings:

Dear Friends, you must proclaim these truths to the world. This is the dawning of a new era; you must not try to conceal it any longer. When you do your duty, God will protect you and the good spirits will watch over you.[xii]

Exhorted by the spirit world to spread the message of their experiences, Kate and her sisters held public demonstrations where they reproduced the rappings and other spiritual phenomena. They sparked a movement that grew like a prairie fire. By the turn of the century in 1900, several million people in the United States and Great Britain had accepted the ideas of Spiritualism as a result of the activities of the Fox sisters and a rapidly expanding number of other practicing mediums.

A small sampling of the list of those who embraced the new teaching reveals such prominent figures as Horace Greeley, the powerful editor of the *New York Tribune*. Greeley was instrumental in ensuring that the message of the Fox sisters was heard. He was the first person to call upon them when they came to New York City, and provided them with protection and societal approval. He opened the pages of his newspaper to the topic of Spiritualism; because of his support, Spiritualists refer to him as the Abraham Lincoln of Modern Spiritualism. Other prominent figures associated with Spiritualism were Professor William James of Harvard University, the father of American psychology; Sir Arthur Conan Doyle, author of the *Sherlock Holmes* mysteries; Victor Hugo, author of *Les Miserables;* Thomas Edison; and Abraham Lincoln, who made use of mediums such as Nettie Colburn for guidance during the Civil War.[xiii]

Spiritualism is the most unique and unusual religion I have ever studied. For one thing, it doesn't have a single charismatic founder or leader. Because it is recognized as having started through the efforts of an eleven-year-old girl, there is no cult of worship surrounding a founder like there is with most religions. Refreshingly, this created an opportunity for the focus of the religion to remain on God.

Secondly, there is no set dogma or doctrine. There is a set of broad principles or guidelines that have been received through mediumship, but even here the Spiritualists recognize that they may have to revise these principles in the future, and have already done so on several occasions. The symbol of Spiritualism is the sunflower. The sunflower was chosen because it moves its face towards the sun as the sun makes its way across the sky. Likewise, Spiritualists attempt to follow truth wherever it may lead. If they find one of their teachings to be incorrect or incomplete as new evidence arises, they know they must discard their old idea and embrace the new one. This is an extraordinary attitude for a religion and very refreshing. One only needs to reflect upon the treatment the ideas of Copernicus and Galileo received by the Catholic authorities of their day to understand how beneficial such an attitude of doctrinal humility can be.

Third, Spiritualism is not just a religion. It is also a philosophy, and a science. It is this embrace of the scientific method that tempers its doctrine. While many religions take a skeptical or even hostile stance towards science, Spiritualism embraces and encourages scientific research into its teachings and spiritual phenomena. Spiritual phenomena have been systematically studied and tested by some of the most prominent scientific minds the human race has ever produced. The long list includes at least three

Nobel Prize winners: Professor Charles Richet, and physicists Pierre and Marie Curie. British scientist Sir William Crookes, who investigated mediums on behalf of the British Royal Society, was also a convinced Spiritualist. Scientific research continues to this day, through the work of people like Professor Gary Schwartz of the University of Arizona, and institutions like the Rhine Research Center in Durham, North Carolina.

29 THE HANDWRITING ON THE WALL

What I am about to describe here is not the telling of a dream or a fantasy, but a fictional example of an occurrence that has happened innumerable times through mediumship.

Imagine a small group of people sitting in a circle in a room. The only light is coming from a lamp with a red bulb. There is a woman sitting in a chair near one corner, but not just any woman. This woman is someone called a *trance medium*. She closes her eyes, and calls upon her spirit guides to work with her. Her head tilts to one side, she slumps into her chair, and appears to be gently sleeping. A wispy whitish substance begins to emerge in front of her. It begins in front of her face. Then it expands and creeps forward and downward, towards the floor, like the vapor created when you drop dry ice in water. It begins to form a whitish pool on the floor at her feet.

The pool begins to rise from the floor like a pillar and slowly forms into the fully clothed figure of a man. The man identifies himself as someone who died years before, and walks around the room giving messages to the other participants. He even touches them and allows them to touch him, and the feeling is of solid substance. The man invites one participant, a doctor, to take out his stethoscope and place it on the man's arm. The doctor does so, and detects a pulse.

After twenty minutes or so, the man dematerializes, and the vapor rearranges itself into the body of a little girl, who visits with the participants, one of whom is her father. When she is finished, her form disappears. The medium awakens from her trance, and the other participants recount to her the events that took place; as a deep trance medium, she has no memory at all of what has just transpired.

The phenomenon described here is called *full body materialization*, and is perhaps the most dramatic physical manifestation from the spirit world that can be experienced on the earth plane. Materializations can also be partial. For example, they sometimes produce only a face, an arm, or a hand. There have been reports of these materializations since prehistoric times, and they continue today.

One of the most well known examples of spirit materialization is found in the Bible. The Book of Daniel recounts the story of what happened to Belshazzar, the King of Babylon, when he misused the sacred vessels that had been pillaged from the Temple of Solomon after Necuchadnezzar's armies conquered Jerusalem in 587 BCE.

"Suddenly the fingers of a human hand appeared and wrote on the plaster of the wall, near the lampstand in the royal palace. The king watched the hand as it wrote. His face turned pale and he was so frightened that his legs became weak and his knees were knocking." Daniel 5:5-6 (NIV)

The hand wrote four words on the wall – MENE, MENE, TEKEL, PARSIN.

The words are recognizable Aramaic, and Daniel interprets them to mean that Belshazzar's reign has been measured by Heaven and found inadequate. Daniel tells Belshazzar that his reign is over and will be divided between the Medes and Persians. That night, Belshazzar is slain, and Cyrus the Great becomes the first ruler of a new empire, Persia. It is from this story that we get the old saying regarding certain fate or destiny – "the hand writing on the wall."

Some of the more famous physical mediums that produced materializations in modern times were Eusapia Palladino, Florence Cook, and Carmine Mirabelli. British medium David Thompson, who currently resides in Australia, is one of the few living mediums that currently travel the world giving public demonstrations of materialization.

30 Science Aids Religion

We are fortunate that the outpouring of spiritual phenomena that began with the Fox sisters in 1848 has taken place in an age when the scientific method of research has been firmly established. Spiritualists themselves were at the forefront of those who were calling for phenomena like materializations to be studied. It is often the case that those of us who exhibit psychic abilities don't know how they happen, and we welcome scientists to use their gifts to aid us in our understanding.

One of the most intriguing questions involves the fact that spiritual entities can affect physical objects. How do spirits produce the sound of a hand rapping on a door or wall, when they have no physical hands? How does a spirit cause a book to move off of a shelf, a picture to fall from a wall, or a piece of furniture to move? How can it be that during a spirit circle, spirits have appeared not just as shadows or vaporous apparitions, but also as solid bodies, whose forms appear human when they are touched? In short, how can a non-physical spirit exhibit physical, material characteristics?

This is one of many puzzling questions surrounding Spiritualism that has been answered through scientific inquiry. The story of the solution to this question provides us with an opportunity to examine an occasion in which science and religion worked together to deepen our understanding of our universe and ourselves. Albert Einstein said, "Science without religion is lame, religion without science is blind." I believe the following story would have made him happy.

During their research in the 1800s, some scientists noticed that a whitish substance would often appear during séances before physical manifestations occurred. Professor Charles Richet gave this substance a name – ectoplasm. After numerous observations, researchers began to suspect that the source of the ectoplasm was the medium. It seemed that this delicate smoky or lace-like substance was being emitted or secreted from the medium's own body. Sometimes it would appear to be coming out of the mouth or nose or other body orifices.

Scientists devised experiments to test this hypothesis. One of them, Dr. W.J. Crawford, who was a lecturer in mechanical engineering at Queens University in Belfast, Ireland in the 1910s. He constructed a device that allowed him to check the weight of mediums before, during, and after spirit materializations. Dr. Crawford would ask a medium to sit in a chair placed on top of a scale. He found that when the medium went into trance and ectoplasmic forms materialized, the weight of the medium dropped. Usually the medium lost about ten or fifteen pounds, but on one occasion Dr. Crawford recorded a weight loss of fifty-two pounds. After the séance, when all materialized forms had disappeared along with the ectoplasm, Dr. Crawford would weigh the medium again and find that all the weight lost during the spirit materializations had returned to the medium.

While Dr. Crawford demonstrated that mediums produce the ectoplasm out of their own body mass, other researchers shed additional light on this unusual substance. Professor Richet was told by a materialized spirit that at the next séance he must bring a pair of scissors. He did so, and the spirit allowed him to cut a six-inch long lock of her hair. Later, he examined the specimen under a microscope, and found that it was actual human hair. Dr. Albert von Schrenck-Notzing of Germany was allowed to amputate a small piece ectoplasm from a materialized spirit. While most of the specimen dissipated like snow, under a microscope the specimen revealed epithelial cells from the mucous membrane. Several doctors have detected heartbeats or pulses from materialized spirits, and upon further examination, determined that the medium was the source of them, even though the medium was seated several feet away from the materialized spirit form.

Photographic evidence revealed that ectoplasm was not only the source of full body materializations, but was also the substance behind other kinds of physical phenomena. Sometimes it would form into ectoplasmic rods that could be used to rap on walls or tables or move objects around, even gripping them and twirling them in the air.

Spiritualists take a rational, scientific approach to psychic phenomena. They don't believe in so-called "miracles" in the sense of being unexplainable Divine acts that operate outside the laws of science. Spiritualists say that a "miracle" is a natural occurrence that we simply haven't discovered the science for yet. As the research that led to the discovery of ectoplasm and its properties demonstrates, even the most mysterious and startling phenomena can be explained and understood once we discover the scientific truths behind them.

For an in depth account of the scientific research mentioned in this chapter, see Arthur Conan Doyle's *The History of Spiritualism.*

31 ABRAHAM LINCOLN HEEDS THE CALL OF SPIRIT

In December of 1862, the Civil War was grinding on with no end in sight. After unimaginable hardships and bloodshed, many soldiers in the Union Army were demoralized. President Abraham Lincoln had recently issued the Emancipation Proclamation in hopes of pressuring the southern Confederate states to abandon their rebellion. It stated that he was planning to liberate all slaves living in any state that had not returned to the Union by January 1 of the coming year. In less than a month he would have to finalize a decision whether or not to go through with his threat.

Lincoln was under tremendous stress. He was having trouble sleeping at night. His wife Mary Todd Lincoln was suffering, grieving over the recent death of their twelve-year-old son, Willie, who had passed away earlier that year on February 20. In an attempt to find comfort, she had taken an increasing interest in Spiritualism, and visited mediums when the opportunity arose.

The nation's capital was heavily populated with military camps. Many wounded soldiers spent their days trying to recover in simple tents, the primitive conditions and cold weather adding more stress to their already weakened bodies fighting to stay alive and heal.

A young lady from Connecticut had a critically ill brother living in one of these camps. Her brother was convinced that his sickness would prove fatal if he couldn't get out of the camp to receive the proper rest and medical attention his condition required. The young lady traveled to Washington with hopes of obtaining a temporary medical furlough for him.

Her name was Nettie Colburn, and she happened to be a trance medium. While Nettie was staying at a house in Georgetown as the guests of a Mr. and Mrs. Laurie, the president's wife, Mary Todd Lincoln, received the news that there was a gifted young medium in town, and requested that Mrs. Laurie arrange a sitting for her. The content of the reading made such a strong impression upon Mrs. Lincoln that she exhorted Nettie to not leave Washington until a meeting with the president could be arranged.

The next evening, a carriage arrived at the Georgetown house, and Nettie was whisked away to the White House. Nervous and hesitant, Nettie nevertheless agreed to go into trance at the urging of the President of the United States, Abraham Lincoln. She immediately came under the control of a male spiritual presence that uttered "almost divine commands." In the presence of several witnesses, including former Congressman Daniel Somes of Maine, Spirit exhorted President Lincoln to go through with the enforcement of the Emancipation Proclamation, urging him to "stand firm to his convictions and fearlessly perform the work and fulfill the mission for which he had been raised up by an overruling Providence."

Nettie prophesied for more than an hour, after which she came out of her trance. Looking around the room in confusion, it took her a moment to remember where she was.

The message having finished, Congressman Somes asked the president, "…whether there has been any pressure brought to bear upon you to defer the enforcement of the Proclamation."

"…It is taking all my nerve and strength to withstand such a pressure," President Lincoln replied.

A few gentlemen then drew around the president and carried out a discussion in low voices, so that others present could not hear. Afterwards, the president turned to Nettie and laid his hand upon her head.

"My child," he said, "you possess a singular gift; but that it is a gift from God I have no doubt. I thank you for coming here tonight. It is more important than perhaps anyone present can understand."

Later, when the time for enforcing the Emancipation Proclamation came due, President Lincoln ignored those urging him to defer it, and went ahead and freed the slaves.

A couple of months later, in February 1863, Nettie gave another reading for the Lincolns at the home in Georgetown where she was staying. After going into trance, Nettie's controlling spirit told the president that the state of affairs at the front where General Hooker had just taken command was perilous and desperate. Others present at this circle described the spirit's message in dire terms— "The army was totally demoralized; regiments stacking arms, refusing to obey orders or to do duty; threatening a general retreat; declaring their purpose to return to Washington."

All those present expressed surprise at the terrible descriptions, except one—President Lincoln.

In a quiet voice he asked Spirit, "You seem to understand the situation. Can you point out the remedy?"

"Yes, if you have the courage to try it," came the reply.

"Try me," said the President, smiling.

With that, Spirit exhorted President Lincoln to immediately go to the front and visit with the soldiers, leaving behind any official entourage, but bringing his wife and children with him. "Inquire into their grievances; show yourself to be what you are, 'the Father of your People.' Make them feel that you are interested in their sufferings, and that you are not unmindful of the many trials which beset them in their march through the dismal swamps, whereby both their courage and their numbers have been depleted."

"If that will do any good, it is easily done," said the President.

President Lincoln was told that he should act as quickly as possible, and broadcast the news of his impending visit right away. In obedience to Heaven's instruction, the president acted immediately; a headline in the Gazette the next morning read, "The President is about to visit the Army of the Potomac."

History records that President Lincoln followed through and visited the troops, lifting the morale of the army, but very few people today know what inspired him to do so.

I was amazed enough when I stumbled upon this account of President Lincoln's daring participation in spirit communication during the most crucial turning points of his presidency. I discovered the story summarized in Sir Arthur Conan Doyle's seminal work, his two volume *The History of Spiritualism*. He in turn had found the story in Nettie Colburn Maynard's memoir entitled *Was Abraham Lincoln a Spiritualist?: or Curious Revelations From the Life of a Trance Medium*, which was published in 1891.

I was much more amazed and inspired when I considered the implications of this story. Not only did Abraham Lincoln exhibit tremendous courage by brushing off the concerns of conventional wisdom that told him there could be considerable political harm done to him if knowledge of his attendance at séances became public, but he also demonstrated a sincere humility in obediently following the advice Spirit gave him at these meetings.

98

As *every* American schoolchild is told, he did boldly enforce the Emancipation Proclamation, leading to the end of slavery and contributing to Union victory in the Civil War. It is also well documented that he visited the troops at the front line and revived their morale.

What *no* American schoolchild is told is the story behind the story, and Sir Arthur has plenty to say about that in his book *The History of Spiritualism*:

This was one of the most important instances in the history of Spiritualism, and may also have been one of the most important in the history of the United States, as it not only strengthened the President in taking a step which raised the whole moral tone of the Northern army...yet the reader might, I fear, search every history of the great struggle and every life of the President without finding a mention of this vital episode. It is all part of that unfair treatment which Spiritualism has endured so long. It is impossible that the United States, if it appreciated the truth, would allow the cult that proved its value at the darkest moment of its history to be persecuted and repressed by ignorant policemen and bigoted magistrates in the way which is now so common, or that the Press should continue to make mock of the movement which produced the Joan of Arc of their country.[xiv]

Sir Arthur's mention of the great French patriot, St. Joan of Arc, is of course a comparison to Nettie Colburn herself, who was not much more than twenty years of age when she was called to perform trance mediumship in front of the President of the United States. Joan of Arc had been just a teenager when, guided by messages from her spirit guides, she convinced the heir to the French throne to allow her to lead his army into victorious battle. Nettie Colburn also demonstrated faith, courage, and humility that are no less noteworthy than that of the President himself.

So this story moves my heart on many levels. Think about this; do you think it is possible for French schoolchildren to be educated without ever hearing mention made of St. Joan of Arc? Do you think it is possible for an Italian child to reach adulthood without ever hearing about St. Francis of Assisi? Is it fair that American children go through their entire education without ever hearing about the story of Nettie Colburn? Of course not! In my view, America's youth suffer from what Victor Frankl called "existential vacuum" in large part because they have been robbed of their spiritual heritage, and this must be corrected if we are to continue as a nation.

Yet there is another aspect of this story that seldom fails to cause me to choke up, tears welling up in my eyes every time I tell it in my public speeches and workshops. It is summed up in the meaning behind one word: Providence.

32 THE SPIRIT OF AMERICA

When in 1636 Roger Williams arrived in what later would become the State of Rhode Island, after having fled charges of sedition and heresy in Massachusetts, he named his settlement Providence, because he had "a sense of God's merciful providence unto me in my distress..."

This word – Providence – has a distinctly American ring to it.

Religion has always played a central role in the story of America. Most people know that at the time of its founding the vast majority of the people in the American colonies were Christian. Nevertheless, in the founding documents of America, you will find no references to Jesus or the Christian faith. You *will,* however, find several references to God. The Declaration of Independence uses the terms "Nature's God," and the "Creator" to refer to the Divine Spirit, and concludes by asserting "a firm reliance on the Protection of Divine Providence." The first two terms are not traditionally Christian, but are closely associated with Deism.

Most of the Founding Fathers were Deists, but they weren't Deists in the way that their contemporaries who fomented the French Revolution were Deist. The French Revolution had an understandably hostile tone towards religion, partly because the interests and power of the French monarchy and the Catholic Church were so closely intertwined. French and other European Deists were far more likely to believe that God took a "hands off" approach to human affairs and history. They believed that while God was the Creator of the Universe, he had only set it in motion and never intervenes in its operation. According to this "clockwork universe theory," God invested intelligence, order, and natural law into his creation as the "Supreme Architect" of the universe, but then walked away from it.

Americans didn't see things the way the Europeans did. There was no widespread hostile perception of religious institutions as tools of the government. Americans were far more comfortable with religion's prominent influence on culture and society than the French revolutionaries were. They believed that God *was* active in their lives and in the life of their nation.

George Washington was the epitome of this tradition. My favorite story about Washington is the testimony of Isaac Potts, a pacifist Quaker resident of Valley Forge who was opposed to the Revolutionary War, who accidentally came upon Washington praying in the woods there:

"...to my astonishment I saw the great George Washington on his knees alone, with his sword on one side and his cocked hat on the other. He was at Prayer to the God of the Armies, beseeching to interpose with his Divine aid, as it was ye (sic) *Crisis and the cause of the country, of humanity, and of the world. Such a prayer I never heard from the lips of man."*

This account of Potts' testimony is contained in the "Diary and Remembrances" of Rev. Nathaniel Snowden, a Presbyterian minister and Princeton graduate, which is on file at the Historical Society of Pennsylvania.

Another story related at a convention of the Connecticut Temperance Union reports that when Abraham Lincoln was asked during the Civil War whether or not God was on the Union side, the president said, "Sir, my concern is not whether God is on our side; my greatest concern is to be on God's side, for God is always right."

In embracing the concept of a God of Divine Providence, I am very American, but I didn't always think this way. When the young man in front of Buffums Department Store in Long Beach asked me, "Do you believe in God?" I replied that I wasn't sure anymore.

I had lost faith in God because there was an inherent contradiction in my theological upbringing. I had been taught that God was Almighty and omnipotent – that he could do anything. Yet as I entered my teens and discovered the incomprehensible level of suffering and violence in the world, it didn't make sense that an all-powerful and loving God would allow this misery and not intervene. I concluded that either God did not exist or he was such a mean uncaring monster that I wanted nothing to do with him.

I had believed that God was either like the God of the European Deists in that he didn't care enough to be involved in human affairs, or he just didn't exist at all. I was angry with that God. I shook my fist at that God.

In the Divine Principle movement, I was introduced to a third possibility that I had never considered. What if God *was* a source of unlimited power and love, but could only manifest that potential when human beings cooperated with him and found the way to *tap into* that power and love?

Here's an analogy. In your home, next to your favorite armchair, there is a reading lamp. It has a working bulb in it, but you can't get it to produce any light when you flip the switch. Miles away there is a nuclear power plant generating an almost infinite amount of electrical power. You might get frustrated and angry because the lamp produces no light, or you might lose faith in the lamp's ability to ever produce light, or you might tell yourself you can live without the lamp and give up on it. Then someone asks you if you are open-minded enough to consider another possibility. You say you are, and this person simply walks behind your chair, picks up a black power cord, and plugs it into an electrical socket in the wall. Just like that, the lamp lights up, brightly illuminating the entire room, as it makes connection to the powerful unseen nuclear power plant.

I had an epiphany like that when I was twenty, and decided to give God another chance. When I did "plug in" to his heart, I found an unlimited source of unconditional love that illuminated my life. If I hadn't been open to making that small step, nothing would have changed.

So getting back to the story of Nettie Colburn and Abraham Lincoln, it moves my heart because it is another demonstration that God had never abandoned the human race. It tells me that he knew of the suffering of the African-American slaves. It tells me that he measured the heart of an Illinois lawyer named Abraham Lincoln and saw something there that made him want to invest his energy into trying to get him elected to the presidency. It tells me that in the depths of Lincoln's agony he saw this sincere man pacing the floor in the White House unable to sleep, lonely and heavy with the weight of his awesome responsibility, longing to know the will of Heaven. God brought a young lady – not much more than a girl – who was full of faith, courage, and humility, to the office of the President. Because of the purity of her heart, God was able to speak through her. The words he spoke through her lips to Abraham Lincoln exhorted him, encouraged him, lifted him up, and strengthened his heart.

As this story moves me my throat tightens and my eyes glisten with tears, because in this story I see the hand of God, I feel the heart of God, and I know the loving presence of God. I know he is there, not just for Abraham Lincoln and Nettie Colburn, but for me and for you as well. He is Divine Providence – the one who provides. All we need do, each one of us, is seek and find the way to plug in our own power cords, to crack open the doorway to our hearts, and let the light of that love come in.

33 FREE TO CHOOSE

Spiritualist Principle #8

We affirm that the doorway to reformation is never closed against any soul here or hereafter.

Spiritualism as a religion is less dogmatic than most. On some issues, when asked what the truth is, it has the humility to simply reply, "We're not sure yet."

Spiritualism offers a set of nine principles. They are not meant to be an immutable creed of infallible doctrines, but simple guidelines for living. Some of them are particularly relevant to the themes discussed in this book, so I will comment on them here.

Christianity is noteworthy for teaching the concept of eternal damnation. When a person dies, they are judged as either having lived according to God's expectations or not, and are subsequently sent to either Heaven or Hell for eternity. All judgments are final!

After 1848, with the explosion of spirit communication that followed the activities of the Fox sisters, mediums began experiencing a very different description of the afterlife than that propagated by traditional Christian doctrine.

In my experience with spirits, I have yet to encounter anyone who was confined to an eternal Hell. I have encountered spirits who were in places that we could reasonably conclude were a type of hell, but there were significant differences. On a few occasions I have met spirits who were reluctant or hesitant to communicate. They were in places I call "gray zones," because there isn't a lot of light there. It wasn't because I wasn't open to talking to them and helping them, it was because something inside of *them* was hindering the communication. I remember one case distinctly.

The spirit stayed at a distance from me, kind of hiding in the shadows, and he was wearing what looked like one of those big scratchy kinds of burlap bags farmers sometimes use to carry produce in. When I was a kid we would use them for sack races at church picnics. He reminded me of the picture of Aqualung on the cover of one of Jethro Tull's albums—crouched over and having no self-confidence.

It was clear to me that this spirit was in this place because *he* thought he should be there. He had hurt people during his life, so he was actually hiding out there because he didn't believe he deserved anything better, and he thought God was probably pretty mad at him.

The fact of the matter is that if this spirit had been willing to accept it, help would have been offered to him, and he could have left this place of darkness, and come into the light. So although you might say this spirit was in a place you might call a hell, it was by no means an eternal sentence, and that whenever he is ready, he will be given the assistance he needs to heal and rise to a more pleasant dwelling place.

It is because of the countless experiences mediums have had regarding the opportunities for forgiveness, growth, and progress in the spirit world, that this eighth Principle was added to the Spiritualist list. The language in this particular Principle was revised as recently as 2001, demonstrating that the learning and adoption of new ideas is an ongoing process in Spiritualism.

34 As a Man Thinketh in His Heart, So is He

Spiritualist Principle #2

> *We believe that the phenomena of Nature, both physical and spiritual, are the expression of Infinite Intelligence*

Spiritualist Principle #7

> *We affirm the moral responsibility of individuals, and that we make our own happiness or unhappiness as we obey or disobey Nature's physical and spiritual laws.*

In these two Principles, we can see that the Spiritualists have a lot in common with Deism and its roots in the Age of Enlightenment. The Declaration of Independence makes reference to "Nature and Nature's God." Spiritualism reflects the Deist belief that everything in the Universe is a manifestation of an Intelligent Creator, but while Deism rejects the concept of "miracles," Spiritualism takes a slightly different view. Deism rejected miracles such as those recorded in the Bible on the grounds that they could not have possibly happened, because our reason shows us that they would have been a violation of scientific or Natural Law. Spiritualism, however, accepts that most of the miracles in the Bible probably *did* happen because many have directly witnessed extraordinary phenomena like clairvoyance, precognition, levitation, visitations from angels, materializations, spirit writing on stone tablets, etc, etc, etc. Convinced that all spiritual phenomena occur within the structure of scientific law, Spiritualism believes that we will eventually discover the scientific basis for all spiritual phenomena, just as the investigation into the nature of materializations and ectoplasm answered many questions about a phenomenon that hitherto had been shrouded in mystery, appearing "miraculous" or "magical."

Beyond explaining physical reality, there are significant implications for our spiritual lives as well. When I asked God to explain human suffering back in the woods when I was twenty-five, he told me, "Those who suffer bring it upon themselves." I have to confess, I could not accept those words at the time. Although it's hard for me to admit it, my subsequent years of spiritual experience have caused my view to come closer to the one God expressed to me back then.

Time and time again, I have seen people bring misery, poverty, and even disease upon themselves simply because of the way they think. Every day, each of us is given countless opportunities to choose between two actions—whether or not to get up for work on time, whether or not to say harsh words to a family member, whether or not to dress properly before going into bad weather, whether or not to eat that donut or pick the veggies instead—and the composite of all these little choices adds up to creating our reality.

It's just like the spirit that insisted on living in the "gray zone" wearing sackcloth even though help was available to him if he ever wanted to improve his situation. We oftentimes create the reality we think we deserve.

Someone thinks, "I'm not smart; I could never take classes to increase my understanding." So they never do.

"I'm really not much of a catch. No person of any substance would ever want to date me." So years later they're in an unhappy marriage.

"Life sucks. It's just way too hard. I'd be better off dead." Surprise! You've contracted a terminal disease.

Although I'm still not convinced it is true in every situation, it's getting harder and harder for me to see a situation where a person's attitude and negative beliefs are *not* creating the reality that faces them. So as every day goes by, I'm seeing this more and more.

The lesson from all this is—police your thoughts! If you think that life sucks, things are stacked against you, and nothing will ever improve, guess what? It'll probably remain true. On the other hand, if you look to emphasize the positive, give out loving energy, and believe in the Divine spark that dwells inside of you, you'll be amazed at the wonderful things that will happen and the wonderful people you will attract into your life. At least that's been my experience, and it hasn't ceased to amaze me every time it happens. It makes for a life of continuous exciting adventure.

Ron Pappalardo

35 DIRECT PROPHECY

When I practice mediumship, I contact spirits who are at different levels in their vibrational state—different stages of development, so to speak. Let's look at these from lowest to highest. On the lowest rung are the *earthbound spirits.* These are people who have lost their physical bodies, yet for various reasons do not ascend into the Light. They hang around on the earth plane instead, sometimes oblivious to the fact that they are "dead"—sometimes stuck here because of some "unfinished business." Sometimes they are confused or afraid they will face terrible judgment or punishment if they ascend into the Light.

A step up from *earthbound spirits* are those who have managed to ascend into the spiritual world, but haven't progressed beyond the *gray zones,* as I mentioned in Chapter 33.

Next come those who have ascended into the Light and occupy a level where they are going through the initial stages of processing their life experience. They might be spending a lot of time just resting, healing from whatever difficulties they encountered in their earthly life. Sometimes they spend a lot of time talking with others about their experiences as they go through a process of gaining greater understanding.

Then there are those who have "settled in," so to speak. They've reached a certain comfort level in their new surroundings, and usually occupy part of their time doing some type of useful work. That may consist of many different possibilities. Some will perform music. Some might enjoy working in the spirit gardens. Others will work welcoming new arrivals into the spirit world or visiting those of us on the earth plane that need assistance. Still others might engage in scientific research, such as looking for cures to diseases, to help those who still dwell on the earth plane.

As pleasant as these places are, there are even higher levels or realms in the spirit world. To obtain entry to these places has nothing to do with any worldly accomplishment or social status attained on the earth plane. The qualification for entry has to do with the content of the heart. Some of the spirits who occupy the higher realms possess a high level of love that deeply moves your heart when you encounter their vibration.

Then, at the highest level, is God himself (or herself, if you prefer—he answers to both Father or Mother). First of all, yes, it is actually possible for you to communicate with God. It is not that complicated, but that doesn't necessarily mean it will be easy to do. This level of mediumship is considered the highest form of mediumship. A great medium of the nineteenth century who is considered the "John the Baptist" of Spiritualism, Andrew Jackson Davis, called this form of mediumship *direct prophecy*. He also referred to it as "the superior condition."

I want to talk more about direct communication with God because, in my opinion, it is the "key to the kingdom." Jesus said a couple of things about the Kingdom of God that are relevant here: *My kingdom is not of this world.* (John 18:36 NKJV) and *The kingdom of God does not come with observation; nor will they say, 'See here!' or 'See there!' For indeed, the kingdom of God is within you.* (Luke 17:20,21 NKJV) Paul taught: *Do you not know that you are the temple of God and that the Spirit of God dwells in you?* (1 Corinthians 3:16 NKJV) In my view, it is only as individuals come to experience communion with God more and more that the kingdom of God will appear. The place "within you" that is the dwelling place of God is your deepest heart. It's not something that can be brought about by political action or public education as it is currently practiced.

A good way to cultivate the sense of feeling God's presence is to practice meditation and prayer. I have had this experience on many occasions, and it is something I can never get enough of. I can describe it as a different state of consciousness. It's not so much a difference in thinking as it is a difference in feeling. I find it hard to put into words; I find it easier to just share the stories of some of my experiences.

One episode involves an experience with spiritual healing. Several years ago I was inspired to go through the training to become a Reiki master. I was performing healings one day when a woman came to me that I knew personally outside of my work as a healer. I knew that this woman had made certain personal lifestyle choices that I had a hard time approving of because of the way I was taught as a child; through the following experience I decided I needed to change the way I thought about this person.

The moment this woman began walking towards me to receive a healing I began to choke up. I felt the Spirit of God come into me, and my perceptive ability became greatly enhanced. I began to have an *empathic* experience, which means I could feel the contents of this person's heart without them saying a word. As I looked at her, I stopped paying attention to the lifestyle choices she had made, not because they weren't true, but because they weren't important to what she needed right then and there from a spiritual point of view.

I knew this person was a mother, and I could feel the love that she had for her child. The spirit of God within me acknowledged the parental love she possessed, and this drew the love of God to her because God, being a parent himself, is moved to see and is drawn towards those of us who express parental love towards our children. As I placed my hands on her, I could feel the love of God pouring through me and into her. Then God said to me, "This is my beloved daughter, in whom I am well-pleased." The parental vibration that God possessed for this woman was the same as the heart vibration this woman had for her child. As this happened, God and I were one. I could feel the unlimited, unconditional love God had for this woman, and *I felt this love for her myself.* The heart of God and my heart became one. I have never looked at this woman since then as anything other than the precious daughter of God. It was such a profound experience, and it changed my life. It made me realize I still had more work to do to keep growing my heart until I reached the same standard that God has.

On another occasion, I was conducting an introductory workshop at the Rhine Research Center. The Rhine is a scientific organization, very scholarly in its approach. Recently God had been coming through strongly in my psychic readings, and I thought I ought to "tone it down" and just present the *factual* information I had. I went to the restroom a few minutes before I was to begin, and God came to me in the restroom. In tears he implored me, "Please tell them about me. This may be the only chance I ever get!" I choked up, and decided to forget taking a purely scholarly approach, and speak from my heart as well. I'm glad I did. Lives were changed that day as some of them got a first taste of the love God had for them on a personal level.

During that period, I was starting to struggle with the way my readings were going. The reason may sound amusing to you. Many people schedule a reading with me because they want to contact their dad, or their Uncle Joe, or some other loved one; they have no expectation that God might drop in. So I found myself feeling I might be disappointing people if they have a Divine experience but never find out how a certain family member is doing.

This came to a head when I did an advanced workshop for the Rhine Center people. The time came for me to give everyone an individual reading, and I was expecting family members and other acquaintances, but God showed up again. I could feel the sense of urgency he had, really longing to communicate with each person. It seems ridiculous to me now, but I actually apologized to the participants, letting them know that I might not get messages from their loved ones because their Heavenly Father wanted to talk to them. One by one, he gave such deep, loving, profound messages tailored to the unique situation of each participant. I was blown away; they were blown away. After he was done talking I felt the energy change, and then we did have a few lesser spirits drop in. I should have known better. I should have trusted him more. No one felt short changed by the experience; everyone seemed deeply moved by what had happened.

This experience was similar to the one I had with the mother I did a healing for. When I was delivering the individual messages from God to each person, I could feel the overwhelming love he had for each one. My heart and his heart merged, and that's the key!

When you connect to the heart of God, and then look at any other human being, you see them the way God sees them. You know you are looking at a unique child of God, an irreplaceable, priceless, one-of-a-kind expression of a particular aspect of God's personality. Unlimited love uncontrollably wells up in your heart towards that person. Just as no two snowflakes are alike, so it is with humans. So each human gives you a unique feeling. The joy you experience seeing them cannot be measured. They appear so beautiful to you, no matter how young or how old or anything else they are.

The mystic Catholic monk Thomas Merton describes having this experience. One day, he had to leave his monastery in the Kentucky countryside to travel to Louisville to take care of some business. While standing on the corner of Fourth and Walnut Streets, he had an epiphany in which he realized that he was one with all people, and saw the tremendous beauty in them, seeing them from God's point of view.

"I suddenly saw the secret beauty of their hearts, the depths of their hearts where neither sin nor desire nor self-knowledge can reach, the core of their reality, the person that each one is in God's eyes. If only they could all see themselves as they really are." — Thomas Merton, *Conjectures of a Guilty Bystander*

The point of all this is that when you have this experience, it becomes impossible to harm another person. God's heart vibration, your vibration, and their heart vibration are all on the same frequency. You are all one. To harm another person would be as painful as harming yourself. In that state, no law has to restrain you from doing harm. No government agency has to send you an e-mail warning you to behave. It just comes naturally.

In my view, that is the coming of the kingdom of God. Not only that. When we become one with the heart of God, we also start becoming one with the mind of God. I know it may sound odd, but we start getting smarter when we connect to God's mind. Ideas and inspirations occur to us more often and about things that have never occurred to us before. We become more enthusiastic. So in these ways also our lives improve.

I have these "heart and mind" experiences often when I am working with people either as a teacher, counselor, or when giving readings. It feels like I enter a higher state of consciousness. When I'm looking into someone's face and I have the intent to give them something that is for their highest good, my heart becomes activated. I feel the arrival of a higher spiritual vibration, and the love I feel for them becomes almost overwhelming. Then it is as if I can sense God is inside of me, looking out of my head, through my eyes, at that person. We are looking at the person together with eyes of unconditional love. For me personally, I can't think of any life experience I have had that is more wonderful, meaningful, and fulfilling as these moments are. If there's any down side to this, on a few occasions when I've taught workshops where I experience this state, I couldn't sleep afterwards. The energy was so high, there was almost a buzzing in the air, and I wound up wide-awake until two or three o'clock in the morning.

It's interesting to note that the word inspiration literally means "to breathe into." It's like the story in Genesis that says God "breathed into" man, "and man became a living being." (Gen.2:7 NKJV) The word enthusiasm means "possessed by God." So don't be surprised that when you get closer and closer to God, you'll grow more and more inspired and enthusiastic.

EPILOGUE

36 THE FLAME YOU CAN'T EXTINGUISH

One Sunday morning in the early 1990s, Connie and I loaded up our kids into the car for a trip to Raleigh; I had been invited to speak at a local church. Joshua loved to ride in the front seat next to me, and Connie didn't mind sitting in the back so our little son could be closer to his dad.

At the church, I delivered a sermon about "building the Kingdom of God" on earth. It was a theme I was talking about a lot when I spoke in those days. After the Sunday Service, we drove back home in the car. Once again, Joshua claimed his favorite place in the front seat next to me.

It was quiet—nobody was talking—when out of the blue he said, "Dad, don't worry if you and the other grown ups can't finish building the Kingdom of God. Me and the other blessed children will finish it for you."

I was amazed. Here was this little boy, so small that his legs just dangled in the air off the front edge of the seat, unable to touch the floor. He was comforting his father, promising to take on the weight of the ages to make a better world. The sincerity and purity of his heart made a deep impression on me that I've never forgotten, and that little episode is one that I often revisit in my memory.

As Joshua grew into his teens and saw how heavy the weight of the world actually was, I think it overwhelmed him. He was fifteen when Osama bin Laden's buddies destroyed New York's World Trade Center towers, and I remember he was so indignant that he told me he wanted to join the army to go fight him. His idealism to make the world a better place was something that was like a flame burning in his heart, even though he didn't know exactly what to do to make it happen.

Then in adolescence, the chemical imbalance in his brain kicked in, and made things even more confusing for him. As he battled with clinical depression, life became a terrifying nightmare.

116

During those last few years of his life, darkness closed in on him, and he lost the battle of trying to keep it at bay.

Nevertheless, when I encounter him now there is no darkness—only light. I have to say I was surprised that his disease did not leave more lasting scars within him. I remember the first long "letter" I received from him after he ascended into the spirit world. The group of spirits called the Council of Light who facilitated the communication described Josh as "… a bright young man, bright as his parents truly know him to be…"

Josh himself was surprised to find that the flame in his heart was still alive:

Dad, I was so surprised to find that my soul was so bright deep inside. I could not believe this was me. I scarcely had a feel for myself in the end, and when I could, I only saw darkness. But that wasn't me.

It may sound strange, but my son and I are closer now than we were those last few years when he was alive on the earth. It's like two tuning forks. You strike only one, but both of them start vibrating. We operate on the same wavelength. So much so that sometimes it's not so clear to me where he ends and I begin. That's not a bad thing; it's actually very comforting.

These days I see that flame or Divine Spark inside of everyone, and it's why I'm full of hope, optimism, and excitement for the future. I believe in people. I'm convinced that all human beings without exception have that Godlike nature within them. No matter how far lost in the darkness someone gets, there is always a point of light available to guide him towards his true self.

In my humble opinion, we are living in an age where, for whatever reason, the veil between the two worlds—spiritual and physical—is becoming thinner and thinner. There is an opportunity for the human race to make a big step forward in consciousness and in the development of the heart. It is a time when more than at any time in our history we can bring heaven down to earth. I'm committed to making the most of this opportunity, and I'm committed to helping you make the most of it, too.

---

[i] My experience visiting the Wimbledon Spiritualist Church can be found in my

first book, *Reconciled by the Light: the After-Death Letters from a Teen Suicide,* in the *Epilogue,* pp. 100-104. You can get a copy here: http://www.reconciledbythelight.com/orderthebook.htm

ii When Spiritualists refer to discarnate entities other than God, they use the term "spirit." When referring to God, they use the term "Spirit" with an upper case "S."

iii You can read about our experience with a *psychometric* reading in *Reconciled by the Light: the After-Death Letters from a Teen Suicide,* Ch. 23, pp. 63-67.

iv Several Bangs sisters paintings reside in a museum at Camp Chesterfield. You can see them by watching a short YouTube video at this internet address: http://www.youtube.com/watch?v=_rYmNnjVHvI Another example of a precipitated painting is the portrait of Our Lady of Guadalupe which was produced in 1531 and now hangs above the altar in the Guadalupe Basilica in Mexico City.

v *Reconciled by the Light: the After-Death Letters from a Teen Suicide,* Ch. 31, pp. 96-97.

vi Genesis 1:26

vii Mark 1:11 English Standard Version

viii If you would like to experience the Sun Meditation, you can download it to your computer from this web address: http://www.reconciledbythelight.com/apps/webstore/products/show/2916329

ix Shapiro, Francine. *EMDR: The Breakthrough "Eye Movement" Therapy for Overcoming Anxiety, Stress, and Trauma.* New York. Basic Books. 1997. Dr. Shapiro's website is: www.emdr.com

x Botkin, Allan L. *Induced After Death Communication: A New Therapy for Healing Grief and Trauma.* Charlottesville, Va.: Hampton Roads, 2005. pp. 10-12. Dr. Botkin's website is: http://www.induced-adc.com/

xi Maharishi Mahesh Yogi, from a seminar of Spiritual Luminaries, Madras, India. 1959.

xii *Educational Course on Modern Spiritualism.* Milwaukee, Wisconsin. Morris Pratt Institute Association. 2001. Lesson 2. pp 3-6.

xiii Colburn Maynard, Nettie ., *Was Abraham Lincoln a Spiritualist: Or Curious Revelations From the Life of a Trance Medium.* Whitefish, Montana. Kessinger Publishing, 2010.

xiv Conan Doyle, Sir Arthur. *The History of Spiritualism,* vol. II. New York. George H. Doran Co. 1926. p.146.

To reach Ron Pappalardo for speaking engagements, telephone sessions, seminars, book signings, or to purchase books, go to www.reconciledbythelight.com

NOTES

NOTES

CPSIA information can be obtained at www.ICGtesting.com
Printed in the USA
LVOW122055160113

315998LV00034B/2228/P